To Keith Wandry

Best wishes,

Harry Farrell
3-10-90

San Jose
—And Other Famous Places

By
Harry Farrell

This limited edition was printed in 1983 as a membership premium by
THE SAN JOSE HISTORICAL MUSEUM ASSOCIATION

635 Phelan Avenue
San Jose, California 95112

ISBN 0-914139-00-2

Printed in USA by
Smith & McKay Printing Co.
96 Santa Teresa Street
San Jose, California 95110

Typesetting and Layout by
Hilary Graphics
San Jose, California

Dust Jacket design by
Graphic Design Service
Junior League of San Jose, Inc.

Limited first edition, 1983
Published by the San Jose Historical Museum Association

TO BETTY
with love

Acknowledgements

Whenever an author begins a book, someone should remind him to keep a list of all who assist the project as it goes along. Not having had such timely advice, I have had to construct my list *ex post facto*. My advance apologies go, therefore, to all whom I miss.

I am especially grateful to P. Anthony Ridder, publisher of the San Jose *Mercury News*, for making available pictures from the newspapers' files. Other picture credits go with thanks to the Associated Press and Bill Regan.

Jerrie Ingram, a long-time and valued friend, deserves special mention for creative counsel in the early stages of the project, not to mention countless hours of typing on the first drafts.

San Jose City Historian Clyde Arbuckle has provided invaluable assistance, coming through time after time for me with elusive bits of essential detail.

I am grateful to Eleanor Fowle and Presidio Press for an excerpt from her biography, *Cranston—The Senator from California*, and to Eleanor also for wise counsel. I thank former President Richard Nixon for permission to use an excerpt from his *Memoirs*; and Eldridge Cleaver for furnishing material from his writings.

I am deeply indebted to my colleagues, past and present, at the *Mercury News*. Due special recognition are former publisher Joseph B. Ridder, Ken Conn, Paul Conroy, Patricia Loomis, Phil Watson,

Dick Barrett, Stan Waldorf, Ben Hawkins, Ben Hitt, Frank Bonanno, Wes Peyton, Dale Lane, Christie Barrie, Bill Feist, John Spalding, John Reed, Sidney Fischer, the late Ralph Condon and Frank Sauliere, and the whole staff of the newspapers' library, including Richard Geiger, Debbie Bolvin, Gene Hoos, Lorene Laffranchi, Chris Larsen, Sally Lowell, Diana Stickler, Bill Van Niekerken, and Elizabeth Walters. Of these, Sally Lowell must be singled out for a special word of appreciation. Under deadline pressure she has been pulling my chestnuts out of the fire for more years than either of us cares to remember.

Because this book is an outgrowth of reporting and column writing over many years, I am immensely grateful to hundreds of news sources, contributors, letter writers, tipsters, and readers. Those whose help is directly reflected in these pages include, in no special order, Audrey Fisher, former Gov. Edmund G. (Pat) Brown, State Treasurer Jess Unruh, Chief of Police Joseph McNamara, Bill Mattos, Bobby Burroughs, Sharon Young, Judge Robert Ahern, Steven A. Walker, Hank Calloway, John Buck, Lick Observatory director Donald E. Osterbrock, Milton Chatton, William Shockley, California poet laureate Charles B. "Gus" Garrigus, Andy Diaz, Sheldon Bayard, Norman H. Moore, Nick Gonzales, Secretary of Defense Caspar W. Weinberger, Sid Burkett, Armand Rynhard, Joan Benedetti, Diane Knaefler, Bob Gross, Mayor Janet Gray Hayes, Ed Steffani, Tevis vi

Dooley, Eldrige Cleaver, County Executive Sally Reed, Clarisa Bernhardt, the late Russ Bernhardt, Jim Berkland, State Sen. Alfred E. Alquist, Helen Blair, Leonora Hering, Jane Blume, Marion Northup, Anna Escobar, Sylvia Jacobson, Curt Bailey, Ethel Bergen, J.W. "Jim" Bailey, Anna Bastian, Florence Schroeder, and the late John P. McEnery.

For certain historical detail I am in debt to archivists of two universities, Linda Long at Stanford and the Rev. Gerald McKevitt, S.J., at Santa Clara.

Last but far from least, I acknowledge with heartfelt thanks the steadfast help of Catherine Healey, a great friend, on the home front during the writing of this book. Without her support in a multitude of crises large and small that have beset me and my family, the undertaking would have been impossible.

Contents

ACKNOWLEDGEMENTS   v

INTRODUCTION   ix

I   GONE ARE THE DAYS...   1
Who remembers Goosetown, Tar Flat, Robertsville, Meridian Corners, or the "Brick Hill?"

II   CHARLIE BIGLEY'S HAT   7
In the era of secret government, San Jose was sometimes run from a garage near City Hall.

III   "HOT DIGGITY-DOG!"   10
Our part of the state has been a lush habitat for political animals—some of them big game.

IV   CHARACTERS   17
The rhyming doc...the Nobel laureate...the woman who talked to God.

V   HAIL TO THE CHIEFS   27
No American president visiting San Jose should take anything for granted.

VI   FROM DEADLINE TO DEADLINE   35
San Jose's pulse is best felt in its newsrooms. The writers there have always laughed a lot.

VII   TYPOS AND BLOOPERS   43
Error-prone words, missing letters, and the perils of juxtaposition.

VIII   STRANGE BEDFELLOWS   48
        When a reporter turns investigator, it helps if he knows whom
        he's investigating.

IX   THE COP SHOP AND THE COURTS   53
        In the police station and the trial courts, one confronts the meanness of
        the town.

X   COLUMNS, CORNICES, AND CONCRETE   59
        Tears were shed when they razed the bastard-baroque City Hall of 1887.

XI   THE SLAUGHTERHOUSE WAR   72
        If the pear orchards had to go, better they were replaced by computer firms
        than stock pens.

XII   YOUNG MAN IN A HURRY   77
        A pleasant rogue, he tried to buy his ticket to immortality. But he bid too low.

XIII   THE MAN WHO TURNED AROUND   81
        In any cause, there is no zealot like a convert. For one, the turnabout has
        been 180 degrees.

XIV   A MATTER OF CONSCIENCE   87
        If the West Coast Japanese were interned for "military necessity," why so
        long a wait?

XV   EARTHQUAKE COUNTRY   91
        It's the imported Californians in whom earth tremors strike terror.
        Natives just shrug.

XVI   THE DECOY HOOKER   97
        Where families once cherished their stately Victorians, street girls, pimps
        and junkies thrive.

XVII   THE TEMPLES OF HIGH-TECH   101
        The would-be D.A. boasted, "I'm the only candidate who knows the difference
        between a computer chip and a potato chip."

        INDEX   109

Introduction

On doctor's orders not too long ago, I reported to the outpatient department of San Jose Hospital for surgical removal of a wart, mole, or some such blemish. The young woman who greeted me sat me down by the desk and began asking the questions that are standard on such occasions. She needed to know my Blue Cross number, Social Security number, vital statistics, next of kin, personal habits, identifying scars—the whole rigmarole.

One question was, "Have you ever been a patient in this hospital before?"

"I was born here," I said. "Does that count?"

"Oh, don't say that," the woman answered, grimacing. "It makes the hospital seem so old."

I cite the incident as a credential for undertaking a book of this sort. In some endeavors, one achieves expertise merely by staying around.

In that connection I set out in 1978, as a stunt for a column, to find the "dean" of San Joseans, the native who had perversely outlived all of his or her original contemporaries and was still here. The dean turned out to be Helen Kamp Allen, a spry woman then going on 103. She had been born at 12th and Martha Streets on April 25, 1875. When I found her she was living in a nursing home only a few blocks from the West San Carlos Street service station where she had spent a fourth of her life pumping gas. She had bought it in 1922 for $900.

"Aunt Helen," as everyone called her, was still a great believer in the cash ethic.

"I've owned 14 houses," she said, "and I never owed a nickel on any of them."

In her century-plus she had held many jobs, starting when she went to work at Hunt's Cannery in Los Gatos at age seven. She had also been a fruit tree grafter, a laundry worker, a hotel chambermaid, a pistol-packing weekend cop at Alum Rock Park, and a real estate entrepreneur. She had had the good sense and foresight to buy nine lots in the Burbank District when they could be had for $100 each and to buy a house downtown, at First and Julian, when it was offered for $300.

Aunt Helen was almost 106 when she died in 1981, having outlived three husbands and both her children. She had been a friend of Leland Stanford and Sarah Winchester. She was one who knew indeed, as we say today, where San Jose was "coming from." There are others like her still around, and many of them unknowingly have contributed to this book. I pick everybody's brains. As a newspaperman, it's my business.

At the time I talked to Aunt Helen, I was little more than half her age, but I got to wondering about my own percentile on the San Jose seniority scale. I consulted an actuary or two, and my findings surprised me. It turned out that even I am well within the top 2 per cent of all San Joseans. My computation (updated for the years that have since elapsed) goes something like this: When I was born toward the end of 1924, roughly midway between the 1920 and 1930 censuses, the city's population was probably about 48,000.* In the ensuing 57 years, as of this writing, the inexorable mortality tables have claimed well over half of those 48,000 persons. And if there are 20,000 survivors, it's a safe bet that more than half of them have moved away. Thus I rank among the top 10,000, seniority-wise, among today's 675,000-odd San Joseans. The rest have followed along after me, by birth, migration, or annexation.

I can claim fairly that three-fourths of my life to date has been devoted to watching the passing scene in San Jose in a more or less purposeful way. I date my journalistic career from the summer of 1939, when (between Hoover and San Jose High) I was tolerated writing obits, church notices, and similar trivia in the old San Jose *News* shop on West San Antonio Street. My remuneration for this duty, eagerly undertaken in the interest of experience, was an occasional pass to one of the South First Street theaters.

I have since covered City Hall, police, courts, politics at all levels, schools, state offices, the North County from Los Altos to Moffett Field, the science and medicine beat, the State Legislature—you name it. I have known the rigors of grinding out a column every day, ready or not. For one brief, long-forgotten period, I was an assistant city editor. The only pages of the San Jose papers that have remained unsullied by my dubious prose are the sports pages.

The seeker of definitive history will not find it between these covers. What is here is a potpourri of fact, folklore, fable, and fun. Two other "f's," fiction and fabrication, are deliberately omitted from the foregoing alliteration, though I must confess that I have supplied certain details of long-ago events from fallible memory. And in a few cases I have invoked Milt Phinney's old tabloid journalism doctrine, which will be found in the "From Deadline to Deadline" chapter. But overall I have taken no serious liberties with the truth. Where exactness matters, I have tried to be exact.

The stories in this book are a motley collection, many never before told. In some cases, notably in "The Slaughterhouse War" and "Strange Bedfellows," I have written "the story behind the story."

---

*San Jose census figures:

1900 – 21,500.	1950 – 95,044.
1910 – 28,946.	1960 – 204,196.
1920 – 39,642.	1970 – 445,779.
1930 – 57,651.	1980 – 636,550.
1940 – 68,457.	1983 (state est.) – 671,800.

If present trends continue, San Jose will pass San Francisco before the next census. San Francisco's estimated 1983 population was 705,700.

Above all, I have tried to keep things on the light side—at least most of the time.

Most of the events related herein could have happened anywhere. The characters are neither necessarily local nor contemporary; the *dramatis personae* range from Leland Stanford to Ronald Reagan, from Eldridge Cleaver to John F. Kennedy. But every chapter reveals something about how San Jose, the Santa Clara Valley, and California came to be what they are.

In no important way is this book autobiographical. An abundance of first person-singular pronouns will be found, but they are only the glue that holds the narrative together.

I am not a San Jose old-timer of the "turn back the clock" breed. It is true, I suppose, that our town was more serene in the blossom-tour era, when our symbol was the prune rather than the computer chip. But what we have lost in the serenity of the "Valley of Heart's Delight" is more than offset by what we have gained in the stimulation and challenge of "Silicon Valley."

Neither am I one who looks back on the growth of the past 30 years and moans, "We botched it." There have been some notable botches, to be sure, about which some caustic words will be found later on. But the remarkable thing about our nine-fold growth since World War II, which has made us the nation's seventeenth largest city, is that we have managed it while retaining an exceptional level of livability.

Recent attempts to "define San Jose" have been in vain. Inevitable adjectives come to mind—"sprawling," "burgeoning," "amorphous," "restless"—all connoting vitality, energy, and change. As long as the change process goes on, San Jose will defy neat pigeonholing as a city of this sort or that, and its identity crisis will remain.

Late in 1981 I took a highly unscientific poll, asking people to name the five best things about San Jose, and the five worst. The top-rated assets were easily predictable: climate, opportunity, recreation, and a rich cultural mix. Neighborhood quality was mentioned; Tony Robinson, an import from San Francisco, said, "You don't have a slum, a ghetto, or anything close to it."

Among liabilities, Mayor Janet Gray Hayes and several others pinpointed a community inferiority complex. As Susan Ager has noted, this is even reflected in our slogan, adapted from the lyrics of our song. It offers no promise but only asks a question: "San Jose—Do You Know the Way?"

But even that slogan represents progress toward self-esteem. In the East Wing of the State Capitol at Sacramento are individual glass display cases for each of California's 58 counties, in which they put their best feet forward, showing off their prime cultural, commercial, climatic, recreational, and other attractions. The exhibits are changed from time to time. When I was covering the Capitol in the 1960s, the best that Santa Clara County's stunted civic mentality could come up with was a display built around a theme that was not only diffident but downright demeaning: "Only 45 minutes from San Francisco."

San Jose of Yesteryear

Sidney Fischer

CHAPTER I
Gone Are The Days...

*The map of San Jose changes constantly. Who remembers Goosetown...Graham Field...
Orchard Street...Rosa Street...Hyde Park...Tar Flat...El Dorado Street...
College Park...Meridian Corners...the "Brick Hill"...Robertsville?*

Our town is a town of Johnny-come-latelys. The fastest-growing place in America has to be a place where a newcomer can become a mover and shaker even before he puts down roots.

Gone are the days when we nurtured our titans, like the Crummeys and the Davieses, by slow, Horatio Alger evolution. Silicon Valley clones its titans instantly now, or imports them.

For better or worse, anyone who has been here five years is an old-timer. Because of a strange civic inferiority complex, we import outsiders to govern us. Too often when a top city or county job opens up, we fill it by a "nationwide search," in the delusion that the best candidate must come from afar—Keokuk, Kalamazoo, or Azusa. We seem to feel bankrupt of worthy hometown talent; a local boy can't make good. The fact that this syndrome has produced as many duds as stars has not vitiated it.

New names, faces, and characters have altered not only our industrial, mercantile, and governmental establishments and our social fabric, but also our habitat. Our fertile fields and orchards have given way to the inevitable sprawl of tracts and shopping centers.

Growth giveth, and growth taketh away. Our map shows new neighborhoods, new landmarks, even new

cities. But vanished from it are many old names that were once cherished parts of our community character.

When San Jose was small, its districts were distinct. Neighborhoods were important, each with its own flavor. None had a zestier flavor than Goosetown.

Goosetown was essentially the old Fourth Ward, south of downtown and west of First Street. In the early 1900s it was marshy, traversed by two creeks that often overflowed, the Canoas and the Guadalupe. The site of the future Woodrow Wilson Junior High School was a pond, and today's West Virginia Street was Pond Street.

Over the decades Goosetown, whose name is virtually gone from our vocabulary, underwent a series of ethnic metamorphoses. The Irish were there, and the Germans. In the first quarter of the century it became a magnet for Italians newly arrived from the Old Country. That was when the Pera family founded the Roma Bakery on Almaden Avenue, which still produces french bread and rolls for the best restaurants in Northern California. Since World War II the Italians have thinned out, and today the neighborhood is mainly Chicano. There is something about the soil, and even the asphalt and concrete, of Goosetown that has consistently produced a hardy breed. Each of its ethnic waves has turned out leaders of the city, of business, of the arts.

The origin of Goosetown's name is open to question. When it was a marsh, some say, it was a stop for migrating geese on the Pacific flyway. That domestic geese and chickens once thrived in almost every backyard is well remembered. But some old-timers insist that the name began in times past when the neighborhood women were constantly pregnant, waddling gooselike with distended bellies.

Life was not easy in old Goosetown. It was a stepchild section of the town—the last, for example to get telephones. So, Goosetowner Hank Calloway remembers, "We resorted to foot, to a hack, or to a bicycle in any crisis, whether we need a midwife, a doctor, a priest, or a fire truck."

It was in Goosetown, at the northeast corner of Willow and Prospect, that my grandparents, the Gallaghers, bought a bungalow when they arrived in California from Kansas about 70 years ago. I lived there for the first four years of my life. One of my earliest memories is of goats pastured across the street, on the south side of Willow, in a field that also served as a playground for Washington School, a block north. The school was a homely, turn-of-the-century structure with a Victorian cupola topped by a flagpole I distinctly remember as crooked. How it got that way I have no idea. Lightning maybe.

The goats were moved out by 1935, when the pasture became Graham Field, San Jose's foremost ball park for some years before Municipal Stadium was built. Its 1,200-seat wooden grandstand cost

San Jose Mercury News

Looking northeast in the early 1930s. Properties marked in foreground would become the site of Civic Auditorium. Old City Hall is in center; still-standing San Jose Museum of Art (then the Post Office) and St. Joseph's Church, left center. Bank of America, upper left, had just been rechristened. It was built in the 1920s as the Bank of Italy. Note that south end of City Plaza is square, not tapered as now.

$9,000 as a project of the SERA (State Emergency Relief Administration), the state-level counterpart of Franklin D. Roosevelt's Public Works Administration. The park was named for the late Jack Graham, who had been pressroom foreman, doubling as baseball writer, for the *Mercury Herald*.* DiMaggio played there. For a dozen years Graham Field drew crowds to night softball, including a bizarre version of the game in which the players rode donkeys. Then late one night in 1947, flames raced through the grandstand, fortunately not in use, consuming it in minutes.

The fire caused no sorrow at City Hall, because it cleared the right-of-way for a needed connection, today's Graham Avenue, which bisects the old ball park diagonally, linking Willow and Keyes streets in a major crosstown artery.

A thoroughfare of Goosetown in its heyday was Orchard Street, whose name, like that of its neighborhood, has faded into history. That name, however, did not succumb merely to diminishing usage; it was stamped out in a surge of civic virtue in 1924.

Orchard Street was a red-light district until its establishments were shut down by City Hall reformers. Having closed the bawdy houses, they determined to go further by getting rid of the street itself. They couldn't rip up the pavement, but they could change the name at least. To what? The *Mercury Herald's* young City Hall reporter Wilson "Bill" Albee (later managing editor) was sitting with the council as it pondered the question. Glancing at the map which showed Orchard Street leading into Almaden Road, he asked, "Why not Almaden Avenue?" Today, the same artery, slightly realigned, is in the process of being converted into Almaden Boulevard, the grand main stem of the Park Center banking district.

In banishing Orchard Street to nominal oblivion, the council was following precedent. In an earlier wave of uplift, the city had chased the whorehouses off El Dorado Street downtown and likewise rechristened it. It has been Post Street since 1902.

In *The Call of the Wild*, the hero dog Buck begins his journey to the Klondike when placed on a train at the College Park station in San Jose. Jack London thus immortalized a North San Jose neighborhood whose name and identity are all but gone (though

---

Herald was dropped from the masthead of the San Jose's morning paper in 1950. The *Mercury* (morning) and the *News* (evening) maintained their separate identities, with combined weekend and holiday editions, until 1983, when both the a.m. and p.m. papers adopted the common *Mercury News* name.

thousands of motorists pass through it every hour on Route 17 where the freeway skirts Municipal Airport).

College Park was a well-defined sector bounded by The Alameda, Newhall Street, the Guadalupe River, and what is now West Taylor Street. It took its name from the Methodist-run College (now University) of the Pacific, which in the 1920s moved to Stockton. The original "COP" campus was taken over by the Jesuits in 1925 and is today Bellarmine Prep.

The College Park Elementary School, at Coleman Avenue and Hedding Street, kept the name of the district alive until it was razed along with most everything else in the southerly approach to the Muni Airport runways. College Park Station, at Emory Street and the Southern Pacific tracks, the one Jack London wrote about, remains as a commuter stop. But of some 44 trains that pass through daily, only a few stop—and not for long; mostly they carry Bellarmine students who live on the Peninsula.

If the padres of an earlier era named their streets for saints, the Methodist founders of the College of the Pacific named theirs for their bishops: Hedding, Emory, Asbury, McKendrie, and Hamline. Of these pious churchmen, it was Bishop Elijah Hedding who was destined to become most famous in San Jose. Fate, abetted by the city planning department, would lift his street from relative obscurity, extend it, and make it a crosstown thoroughfare, not to mention the main artery of our Civic Center.

Originally, Hedding dead-ended on the east at the Guadalupe River. On the other side of the stream was a vegetable patch extending all the way to North First Street, purchased by the city and county in 1948 as the first Civic Center parcel. Then the site was referred to as "First and Rosa," because Rosa Street, which happened to be in line with Hedding, led eastward from First. As the Civic Center took form, Rosa and Hedding were linked up across it, with a new bridge over the Guadalupe, and Hedding won out as the name for the whole thing. This was probably just as well, for the name Rosa never had much legitimacy in the first place. Rosa Street was named for Rosa White, an antebellum belle in Milledgeville, Georgia, who as far as anyone knows never got any closer than that to San Jose. She happened to be the sister of Thomas White, our city surveyor in about 1850, who sentimentally memorialized her for a hundred years in our street grid.

Of course, there is no record that Bishop Hedding ever came to San Jose either. Just as his posthumous fame grew, Bishop Hamline's shriveled. Hamline Street, parallel to Hedding and north of it, was the original main route between College Park and North First Street, with its own bridge across the Guadalupe. But one section of Hamline was knocked out by

San Jose Mercury News

Until the mid-1930s, Southern Pacific's main line tracks ran down Fourth Street, jamming traffic on East Santa Clara Street (above) and other east-west arteries.

the Route 17 Freeway and another by the Civic Center. The bridge was dismantled, and today only a vestige of the street remains.

(Coleman Avenue, the main north-south street through College Park, has nothing to do with the Methodists. It was part of Locust Street until the late 1930s when it was renamed for Hugh C. Coleman, a popular gym teacher at the old Roosevelt Junior High, who was killed in a fall on the school floor.)

At Hamline and First Streets, about where the County Social Services Building is now, was the placid village of Hyde Park. Though less than two miles from the heart of the city, it retained a quasi-rural atmosphere until 1960, when it was gobbled up by the northward expansion of the Civic Center. The 1952 City Directory listed no fewer than 10 stores with "Hyde Park" names, including a food shop, a beauty parlor, a tavern, a drugstore, a hardware store, a garage, and a service station. Today the name survives only on a grocery and a liquor store.

A few blocks southeast of Hyde Park was the northern counterpart of Goosetown, a neighborhood of sturdy working-class families who called the place they lived Tar Flat. It was the old Second Ward, centering around Tenth and Julian Streets. Tar Flat

is still there, though few of today's residents would recognize the name, which long ago dropped from sight and sound. Not even City Historian Clyde Arbuckle knows where the name came from. I once inquired about it in my column and got two widely divergent responses. Ray Mathewson, whose father was a Second Ward councilman sometime before 1916, said the name was derived from a sticky, ill-smelling tar weed rampant throughout the area. Other readers insisted that "Tar Flat" reflected the fact that the town's four or five black families lived there. In that age of innocence San Joseans failed to see any evil in racial imagery.

Far across the Valley from Tar Flat, another name from yesteryear has vanished. Few who hawk or buy Cadillacs, Buicks, Volvos and Toyotas on Stevens Creek Boulevard's auto row are aware that today's clogged intersection of Stevens Creek with Saratoga Avenue, well into the post-World War II era, was a sleepy country crossroads called Meridian Corners. Not much was there, amid the orchards, except two saloons, a grocery, and a blacksmith's forge.

Why "Meridian Corners?" Again, no one seems to have the answer. What is certain though is that Meridian Corners had no relationship to Meridian Road (now Avenue) running south from Park Avenue to Willow Glen. Meridian Avenue takes its name from the fact that it follows the north-south map line passing through the summit of Mt. Diablo, which is the base point for real estate surveys throughout the Bay Area. The road was laid out in 1852, but it was found to be cockeyed because the original surveyor had used magnetic compasses and magnetic north kept changing. In a new survey in 1889, help was sought from the astronomers at Lick Observatory, which had opened the previous year atop Mt. Hamilton. Astronomer James Keeler set up a bull's-eye lantern on the south edge of the old county fairgrounds, where Meridian takes off from Park Avenue today. Two thousand feet south he erected a stone monument on which he set his transit. Sighting on the North Star, he determined that the original road deviated from the meridian by about eight feet per half-mile, enough to cast a cloud on every land title in the area. The correction was made, and Meridian Road became an honest north-south line.

There used to be other "corners" all over the Valley. The crossing of Lawrence Station Road (now Lawrence Expressway) with El Camino Real was Milliken Corners. A little farther up El Camino, where it turns at the convergence of Wolfe Road and Fremont Avenue, was Butcher's Corners. The turn on Fremont, where it now intersects Foothill Expressway, was Loyola Corners.

Three other Santa Clara Valley villages that passed into nominal oblivion were Robertsville, Alma, and Mayfield.

Until long after World War II, Robertsville was a place of distinct identity and rural flavor on the road to Almaden. It took its name from John Griffith Roberts, who farmed 500 surrounding acres in the late 1800s. It has given way to the thriving shopping district (Food Villa, Orchard Supply Hardware, etc.) at Almaden and Branham. (Quaintly, the San Jose Post Office refers to its substation on Branham Avenue as the "Robertsville Station.")

Alma was a bustling hamlet on the road to Santa Cruz, above Los Gatos, until midcentury. It boasted, among other enterprises, a railroad station, a general store, a tavern, and the area firefighting headquarters of the State Division of Forestry. Today not a trace of it remains. Lexington Dam, built in 1952, inundated it; and now whenever the reservoir is full, sailboats glide where the fire rigs roared.

It took a bit of horsetrading at Sacramento, incidentally, to get the low-level road through Alma moved farther up the hillside so that Lexington Dam could be built. A $2,475,000 appropriation to reroute the highway bogged down in the State Senate. At about the same time the formidable Sen. Randolph Collier of Yreka (the "Father of the Freeways") was trying to raise the gasoline tax to finance the freeway system we know today, but his measure, bitterly fought by the oil lobby, was having trouble in the Assembly. The late Assemblyman (later Senator) John F. "Jack" Thompson of San Jose swapped his vote for the gas tax for Randy Collier's support of the road-moving bill. So both became law.

Mayfield was a rootin'-tootin' sin town in northern Santa Clara County that vanished because it guessed wrong. Its main attractions in the 1880s were its saloons, which were many. That was when Sen. Leland Stanford was building his university on his farm a little to the north. He went to the Mayfield people with a proposition: If they would dry up their community, he would designate it the home city for his school and make it flourish. But the saloonkeepers turned the senator down; they thought booze offered surer prosperity than academe. So Stanford established his new university town on the green fields farther north, calling it College Station. It evolved into Palo Alto, which in 1925 swallowed Mayfield whole. Mayfield is now Palo Alto's California Avenue business district. The old name lingers on at Mayfield Mall, but that is really further south in Mountain View, and at this writing it is due to shut down within a year.

Palo Alto maintained a dry zone around Stanford University well into the 1960s. Early students (Herbert Hoover among them, perhaps) often walked miles to Mayfield to partake of its forbidden pleasures, a practice immortalized in a bit of campus doggerel by Leroy Ladd, '07:

> Oh, there's a road to Mayfield,
> As plain as plain can be,
> And if you want to see a wreck,
> Just take a look at me;
>
> For I have been to Mayfield
> And tasted of the beer,
> And that is why my eyes are weak —
> I need to rest a year.

Not only names, but also prime landmarks have disappeared from our map, our terrain, and sadly, almost from our memory. There was, for example, the "brick hill."

If a yellow brick road led to the enchanted Emerald City of Oz, a red brick road led to many an enchanted afternoon for pre-World War II generations of San Joseans. The "brick hill" was a picturesque mile of Alum Rock Avenue below the San Jose Country Club. Driving over it made tires sing. The bricks are still there, actually. But a few years after the war they were paved over with grim, gray asphalt. A bit of the adventure in a picnic trip to Alum Rock Park thus vanished forever.

Across the Valley, Lone Hill remains as a place name, borne by a school and a park on Harwood Road south of Branham Lane. But the geographical feature from which they take their identification is no more. Lone Hill was a commanding landmark amid the vineyards southwest of San Jose: not just a gentle rise but a small solitary mountain jutting up from the Valley floor. It was visible for miles until it was bulldozed and quarried away. What is left of it isn't worth the name.

The vanished vocabulary of bygone generations was not always on the map. Sometimes it was in our spoken and written idiom.

A San Josean may think of himself as an old-timer if he recalls our telephone exchange names before 1962, when Pacific Telephone got rid of word prefixes and went to all-digits in a change that many considered dehumanizing. But if nostalgia engulfs you with CYpress, CLayburn, AXminster, ELgato, REgent, WHitecliff, and YOrkshire, think about "Ballard," "Columbia," and "Mayfair." Those were the magic words essential to the completion of San Jose phone calls before the advent of dialing in 1949. The caller lifted the receiver and waited for "Central" to ask, "Number please?" and then told her the number wanted. ("Central" was always a woman.) Seven-digit numbers had not arrived yet. Most people had four digits followed by J, W, R, or M, thus: "Ballard 2521-J." (Even Bob Brown, Pacific Telephone's man in charge of such things, has never been able to find out where "Ballard" came from.)

A short number or a number ending in two or three zeroes was a status symbol and in some cases a business asset. The city manager's office (we had no mayor) was Columbia 1; the city clerk was Columbia 3. The *Mercury Herald* was Columbia 600.

Residents of the East Foothills had exclusive Mayfair numbers; to many, the East Side is still the "Mayfair District." Actually, telephone service there remained relatively primitive almost into the 1940s. As late as 1937 Dorothy Larocca on Claremont Avenue shared her line with nine other parties. A four-party line was a luxury, and the only one-party lines on the East Side were for doctors and public officials.

(Phone service here, however, had long since lost the easy informality remembered by former *News* reporter Patricia Loomis from her girlhood in Arroyo Grande, around 1930. "The phone was on the wall," she says. "I'd pick up the receiver, turn the crank, and say, 'Hi, Blanche, I want to talk to Aunt Muriel.' And Blanche, the operator, would get her for me. Or I'd say, 'Blanche, do you know where my mother is?' And Blanche would find her.")

Sporadic efforts to make sense of our erratic street name pattern have driven a lot of nomenclature into history. The campaign for consistency still has a long way to go; Gertrude Stein's "rose is a rose is a rose" makes considerably more sense than "Alum Rock Avenue is Santa Clara Street is The Alameda is El Camino Real," but both are equally true.

Rosa White of Georgia is not the only person who had her commemoration in the San Jose street grid posthumously obliterated. In her banishment she stands in good company, with, among others, St. Augustine and C.B. Polhemus, the latter a builder of the first railroad from San Jose to San Francisco.

What was Polhemus Street until the 1960s is now that part of West Taylor between The Alameda and the Guadalupe River. Its name was changed when it was angled to link up with Naglee Avenue. At the time there was talk of renaming Naglee too, so that the whole artery from east to west would be Taylor Street; but with regard to Naglee, which memorializes

a Civil War general from these parts, tradition won out. (Adding to the confusion is the fact that Naglee Avenue is clear across town from Naglee Park, the once prestigious residential area now sadly identified as the "mental health ghetto" of board-and-care homes east of San Jose State University.)

In another link-up, the name of St. Augustine was stricken from our downtown map when San Augustine Street was twisted slightly to join St. John Street at Market. They are now West St. John and East St. John respectively.

Yesteryear's maps also show Whitney, Priest, Crittenden, Clay, Webster, Jones, Monroe, and Adams Streets on the East Side. They are still there but known respectively today as 12th, 14th, 16th, 19th, 20th, 21st, 22nd, and 23rd Streets. Consecutive numbering of San Jose streets early in this century stopped at 11th. From 11th to the Coyote Creek, north-south streets were alternately named and numbered. When the names were dropped, the numbers were shifted to fill in the gaps, so that, for example, today's 17th Street is the old 14th.

East of the creek, in what until 1911 was the separate City of East San Jose, all the north-south streets had names, not numbers. After San Jose annexed its eastern neighbor, however, the council decided it would lessen confusion if all the north-south streets were numbered in order. One vestige of the old East San Jose name pattern remains: south of William Street, 24th Street is still McLaughlin Avenue all the way past Capitol Expressway.

Two other hardy street names that have refused to bite the dust are Bird and Montgomery, designating portions of the same thoroughfare that meanders from the northwest industrial district through Palm Haven and into Willow Glen. At a meeting about 1950, the city planning commission tried vainly to impose a single name on this artery but could not decide between Bird and Montgomery. As it happened, a delegation of Italians was present on another matter, seeking to have Christopher Columbus commemorated by some physical feature of the city. (They finally brought about the naming of Columbus Park.) But before that was done, commissioner Larry Appleton thought he had a compromise that would solve two problems at once. Looking at the erratic route taken by Bird and Montgomery Streets, he asked, "Why not call the whole thing Columbus Boulevard? Columbus didn't know which way he was going, either."

CHAPTER II
Charlie Bigley's Hat

In the era of secret government, San Jose was sometimes run from a garage across the street from City Hall.

Behind the scenes at San Jose City Hall there have always been murky figures reputed to exert inordinate influence over the happenings there.

One might tick off a list including Al Ruffo, the high-powered lawyer; Terry Christensen, the political professor; bridge builder Dan Caputo; engineer Chuck Davidson, the rezoning whiz; and others of many ilks. In the 1950s and '60s, *Mercury News* publisher Joe Ridder worked the levers of municipal power in concert with the late City Manager A.P. "Dutch" Hamann.

But San Jose's last political boss in the classic mold—kindred of Tweed, Hague, Crump, Pendergast, and Daley—was Charlie Bigley. In the late 1930s he was the man to see for a favor or, more pertinent in that Depression decade, a job. The "Bigley Machine" ran City Hall.

The essential difference between Bigley and other string-pullers over the decades was the source of his clout. The influence of Ruffo, Davidson, and others, derives from their connections, properties, talents, or services. Bigley's power flowed, albeit via unconventional channels, from the people.

He had started poor in the early part of the century delivering a bakery route, dispensing favors along with the bread, notably to other poor folk and the immigrants in places like Goosetown. And he was a hustler. He opened a cigar store near the old Southern Pacific Depot on Bassett Street. Then he started a taxi company, with a sideline of renting mourners' cars for funerals; this evolved into the Bigley Ambulance Company (which is still around, under other management). By the '30s Charlie was wealthy with his ambulances, a partnership in a liquor firm, an auto storage garage on South Market Street (convenient to the old City Hall in the Plaza), and a palatial home on The Alameda, the scene of fabled political barbecues.

His other love, besides politics, was children. If he saw a kid yearning for a toy in a store window, he'd go in and buy it. Sometimes he would buy up a whole stack of papers from a newsboy. Clark Bradley remembers, "He'd buy 50 or 60 pairs of children's shoes and give them away. That was almost an annual event."

Bigley was a rugged man who could and did sling liquor cases onto his trucks with the best of his men. The few extant photos of him suggest power as well as paunch, geniality mixed with square-jawed toughness.

He took over City Hall by the rule of "select and elect." Favors he had bestowed in his rising years made him a father figure to thousands, who would mark their ballots as he told them. So, in each city election, he would *select* a slate of candidates and then, with his faithful, *elect* them. This worked so well that for years at least four of the seven council members

"Dutch" Hamann: the levers of power.

were always "Bigley men," who would often gather in the Bigley garage before meetings to settle whatever business was coming up. Then they would cross the street to City Hall to make it official.

The city manager then was Clarence Goodwin, a handsome, silver-haired Presbyterian elder who exuded dignity and probity. He also had a sure instinct for political survival and understood that since he held his job at the sufferance of the council, he also held it at the sufferance of Charlie Bigley. Goodwin, with Bigley's assent, ran a taut ship at City Hall, a lean operation stingy with tax dollars. Used trucks were bought for the city's Depression-era WPA force. They had to cost under $500 so they could be acquired without bids.

Bigley certainly invoked his clout in his own interest, notably the furtherance of his ambulance business, which needed a friendly police department. But mostly he cherished power for the sheer joy of it and his control over patronage. If he wanted you to have a city job, there was always a way to short-circuit civil service hiring rules. Well into the third quarter of the century there were those in lofty status who owed him

their careers, one being longtime Chief of Police Ray Blackmore. Bigley told Goodwin to hire Blackmore as a rookie cop in 1929 because he thought Ray was a hot prospect for the department's ball team.

Though Bigley was a benign boss, the very fact of his bossism outraged purists (and of course losers). So, as his power grew, so did the ranks of his enemies. His power waned in a series of "throw the rascals out" movements in the late 1930s and early '40s, and about the time I took over the City Hall beat as a cub reporter in 1946, he died of cancer at age 57. Thus I never met him, but there was an unsuspected link between his regime and my reportage.

Bigley's memory was still fresh and evoked emotions ranging from affection to awe to dread to contempt among the denizens great and small whom I encountered at City Hall. Most of them worked there either because or in spite of him. I heard a lot of Bigley lore, and with good reason I always listened in owlish noncommital to the outpouring of the legend.

I was wooing my wife-to-be, Betty, then and was newly aware that her mother, Maude Regan, was a cousin to Mary Bigley, the boss's widow. It further

Charlie Bigley: last of the bosses.

turned out that his head size had been 7, the same as mine, and when Mary was disposing of his things, she gave his best hat to me—an expensive one, brown.

Thus it came to pass that for six years after the boss was stowed in his crypt in Oak Hill Mausoleum, his hat was still making daily rounds of his old domain, City Hall—on my head.

I discovered early that in governmental reporting, an incessant battle rages between the media, whose job it is to ferret out facts, and the officeholders and bureaucrats with their natural penchant for secrecy. In California, reporters now have on their side the Ralph M. Brown Act (named for a one-time Assembly speaker) requiring most public bodies to conduct their business in the open.

Before it was passed in 1953, however, public officials got away with murder. In the early post-Bigley years, the City Council met officially at 8 o'clock each Monday evening. But the shots were called earlier, as councilmen gathered at 7 in a small room off their chamber to chew over their agenda behind closed doors and reach decisions on most items. Only formal ratification, often with little or no debate, remained for the regular, public session.

We reporters had two options for dealing with the star-chamber meetings—a Hobson's choice, really. If we gave our pledge not to print anything we heard, we were allowed to sit in for "background" only. Or we could boycott the closed meetings and stay free of ethical restraints, relying on leaks to find out later what was going on. I tried it both ways and finally settled on the boycott as preferable to the gag rule. I could always find at least one spy on the council, willing to give me a *sub rosa* fill-in.

The secret sessions, which obscured the councilmen's motives, protected their images as well. One such case occurred in the late 1940s when the first city sales tax was being considered. A certain councilman, something of a snob, was wailing about the heat he was taking on the issue. His memorable utterance, which never saw print because we were honor-bound to ignore it, was, "People are really mad about this. And I mean responsible people, too—not just the working class."

CHAPTER III
"Hot Diggity-Dog!"

*Our part of the state has been a lush habitat for political animals—some of them big game.
One left a wide concrete trail across the San Jose terrain.*

One evening in the mid-1950s I went out to the University of Santa Clara's old "Ship" theater, long since razed, to cover a speech by the late Gov. Goodwin J. Knight. A superb off-the-cuff speaker, he regaled an audience of students and professors for an hour and then opened himself to questions.

This was long before the time of campus turmoil; undergraduate heckling of visiting dignitaries was never dreamed of, let alone condoned. On this occasion, however, the governor found himself floundering in the face of intelligent, incisive questioning by a freshman in the third or fourth row. This intense, dark-haired youngster knew much more about what was going on in Sacramento than one would expect. On some matters he was clearly better informed than the governor.

After the program the jovial Knight, a Republican, continued his give-and-take with a knot of students who crowded around him backstage, including the inquisitive young man who had enlivened the evening out front.

"Who's that kid, anyway?" I asked somebody.

"Oh, him? He's Jerry Brown," I was told.

The future governor's political interest reflected the fact that his father, Edmund G. "Pat" Brown Sr., who was then state attorney general, was preparing to challenge Knight for the governorship in the next election.

Jerry Brown would retain a close affinity with Santa Clara County. He would soon quit SCU, however, to begin preparation for the Jesuit priesthood at the Novitiate overlooking Los Gatos. For three years he led a cloistered existence there, doing menial chores including cleaning toilets (he once told me) and picking tons of grapes, praying and meditating for hours, and studying Latin, Greek, philosophy, and religion. He was allowed off the premises rarely. Once he was taken to a dentist in Los Gatos, and he received special permission to attend his father's inauguration as governor in 1959.

Finally, feeling out of the tide of human events, he left the novitiate to pursue a secular career in law and politics. What effect his three remote years on the Los Gatos hillside had on his later life has been often conjectured but can only be guessed.

If Ronald Reagan is the best political orator to arise out of California, "Goodie" Knight was probably the best political raconteur.

A buoyant extrovert, he first went to Sacramento in 1947 as lieutenant governor under Earl Warren. He became governor by succession in 1953 when President Eisenhower named Warren chief justice of the United States. Knight had hoped to move up to the governorship five years earlier, however, when Warren was the Republican nominee for vice president, running with Tom Dewey against Harry Truman.

Seminarian Jerry Brown, in clerical collar, was given rare permission to leave the Novitiate at Los Gatos to attend the inauguration of his father, Gov. Pat Brown, in 1967. Joining him behind his parents are sisters Kathleen, Cynthia, and Barbara.

That was the race that ended in the upset of the century when Truman was re-elected after virtually all pundits had written his political obituary.

Naturally no one more wanted Dewey to win than Knight did, for then Warren would go to Washington and Knight would become governor. The campaign gave rise to a yarn Knight used to tell with zest.

On the last weekend before the election, so the story went, the Republicans held a massive rally in Los Angeles, at someplace like the Coliseum, with thousands present. Dewey and Warren were both there, as were all western Republican leaders including, of course, Lt. Gov. Knight. The event broke up in a great surge of optimism, with the Republicans certain that on the ensuing Tuesday they would recapture the White House, from which they had been shut out for 16 years.

Train travel was still common then, and after the rally Knight headed for the station to catch the Southern Pacific's old "Lark" back to Northern California. In a warm, expansive mood, he decided to have a fine dinner before retiring. He started making his way back through the cars to the diner.

Somehow Goodie got into a file of mental patients being transferred between state hospitals. Their attendant had stationed himself at the entry to the dining car, counting off his charges as they came through: "...seventeen...eighteen...nineteen..."

At that point Knight came along. The attendant, not recognizing him, asked, "Who are you?"

Goodie, who was stocky and not too tall, pulled himself up to full height and replied sonorously, "Sir, I am the next governor of California!"

Tapping him on the shoulder, the keeper resumed

San Jose Mercury News

Shirt-sleeved Gov. "Goodie" Knight takes time out during a San Jose visit to sign some bills before the deadline.

counting: "...TWENTY...twenty-one...twenty-two...etc."

A better-documented story, a classic in State Capitol press lore, grew out of Knight's actual succession to the governorship later. When word came in on the press room teletypes that Gov. Warren had been named chief justice, several reporters dashed for the lieutenant governor's office to give Knight the news and get his reaction. They were expecting some high-flown if banal rhetoric, but Knight's response was nothing if not sincere: "Hot diggity-dog!"

That effervescent answer produced an echo years later during Pat Brown's governorship. Pat was hosting the National Governors Conference in the then brand new Century Plaza Hotel in Los Angeles, and he was proud of his state. As a hospitality gesture, he chartered a jet to give his fellow chief executives a scenic overview of California from one end to the other. The idea was, they would fly north over the Monterey Peninsula, the Golden Gate, and Pat's Capitol in Sacramento; after circling Mt. Shasta, they would return over Lake Tahoe, Yosemite, Death Valley, and fertile farmlands.

In the conference press room a few of us got to discussing, quite seriously, the wisdom of this flight.

"Suppose that plane with all 50 governors aboard would crack up," someone said. "State government would come to a standstill all across the nation."

Bob Houser, political editor of the Long Beach *Press-Telegram* spoke up. "No," he said, "if that plane went down, I'll tell you what would happen. All over the country, you'd hear 50 lieutenant governors shouting in unison, 'Hot diggity-dog!'"

(That Governors Conference, by the way, produced another memorable vignette. Hollywood had gone all-out to entertain Pat's visitors, offering, besides many stars in the flesh, the premiere of a new movie, *How to Steal a Million*. One eastern governor, reading the convention program, found the title intriguing until he realized it was just a motion picture. "Oh, is that all?" he said. "I thought it was a seminar.")

A political character who left his visible mark on San Jose while rising to world renown is Pierre Salinger. He also spent some time in our county jail—not the infinitely bad one we have now, but its predecessor, a box-like 19th-century structure that was infinitely worse.

Salinger, who would become President Kennedy's press secretary and later a sort of unofficial Voice of America on French television, demonstrated his showmanship flair early, as a reporter on the *San Francisco Chronicle*. About 1950 he was assigned to investigate conditions in a number of California jails; so he connived with judges to have himself incarcerated in them incognito. The San Jose jail was one of the lock-ups he thus penetrated. His resulting exposé made a big splash; *Chronicle* rack cards all over Northern California touted it with the provocative title "ALIAS PETER FLICK" in stud-horse Gothic.*

From reporting, Salinger drifted into political press-agentry. I first encountered him as press secretary to Richard Graves, the Democrats' long-forgotten candidate for governor in 1954. "Plucky Pierre" had a string of losers before he hit a winner, Kennedy.

It was in the tumultuous year following Kennedy's assassination that Salinger left his monument in concrete and steel, the bold slash of Interstate 280, across the face of San Jose. Without him, it might not be finished yet.

As a holdover from Camelot, Pierre was uncomfortable in Lyndon Johnson's White House. So, sud-

---

*"Stud-horse Gothic": A style of huge, black block letters once favored by horse breeders for posters advertising the services of sires; also called "Second Coming type" by some old-time editors, who counted on using it for their headlines on Judgement Day.

denly, in a move that rocked the Democratic Party, he quit to fly home to California and file for the seat of U.S. Sen. Clair Engle, then dying of cancer. Many felt he stole the nomination from Alan Cranston, the favorite of most party pros. (Cranston would have to wait four more years to become a senator.)

Within weeks after the primary, Engle died, and Gov. Pat Brown appointed Salinger to fill out the term, so that he would have "incumbent" after his name on the November ballot. As an instant senator, Pierre needed desperately to demonstrate some clout during the fall campaign. He turned for help to the new president, Johnson, who owed him a favor for seeing him loyally through the transition from the Kennedys.

The favor LBJ bestowed was characteristic of the old Texas pork-barreler. He sprung loose a big appropriation (the figure that sticks in my mind is $87 million) to give Salinger something to point to; it was to complete Route 280 across San Jose. Until then the project had been bogged down in interminable controversy.

Today 280 stands as perhaps the only tangible evidence on the face of the state that Salinger, reporter-turned-P.R.-man-turned-politician, was indeed California's junior U.S. senator for a few months in 1964. But Johnson's gesture came to naught politically; Salinger's candidacy had splintered the Democratic Party in California; Cranston loyalists sat on their hands during the fall campaign. Pierre lost it to his Republican opponent, movie song-and-dance man George Murphy.

Ever loyal to the Kennedys, Salinger re-entered the arena a mainstay of Robert Kennedy's attempt to capture the White House in 1968. But again assassination—Sirhan Sirhan's bullet—cut short Pierre's political career. He has never returned to it.

Estes Kefauver, the coonskin-capped senator and crime-buster from Tennessee, was in and out of the Bay Area often in 1952 and 1956, running for president (and finally for vice president on Adlai Stevenson's ticket). He had a deeply personal campaign style; he endeavored with considerable success to project himself as the great and close individual friend of every voter. The towering senator was especially good with the elderly; he would clasp the frail hand of an old lady, gaze soulfully into her eyes, and she would be his forever. But too often, his neglect of homework showed.

Part of Kefauver's standard performance in each town he visited was to mount the platform of a bunting-draped truck outside his store-front headquarters and tell the people how he dreamed of someday (presumably after his presidency) quitting politics altogether.

Bernard Charlon

Pierre Salinger: a guest in our slammer.

"Sometimes I think I'd just like to settle down and practice law," he would say, "and I can't think of anywhere I'd rather do it than (fill in name—San Jose, Sunnyvale, Watsonville, or wherever)."

Then, as his spiel continued, Kefauver would pay glowing tribute to his local supporters, proclaiming them his dearest friends. In 1956, two of them in Santa Clara County were lawyer John Thorne and scientist Sid Tetenbaum, upon whom he lavished long and flowery praise. But he blew it, calling them John *Thorpe* and Sid *Tannenbaum*.

Kefauver's campaigns, though colorful, were understaffed, ragtag, accident-prone operations. Once he even pressed me into service to extricate him from chaos.

He had been stumping in San Jose all morning, and his last stop was at the FMC plant on Coleman Avenue. There he donned a crash helmet and white duster and rode around the test track in one of FMC's famous amphibian vehicles. Then his motorcade

Estes Kefauver in San Jose; he barely made it to Santa Cruz. At left, David Friedenrich and Mrs. Kefauver.

headed for Santa Cruz, the senator riding in an open Cadillac flying American flags from the fenders.

The freeway, Route 17, was still years in the future, and the cars had to wind through a grid of San Jose streets to get onto the old, two-lane San Jose–Los Gatos Road. Alas, the tour had been set up by a San Francisco P.R. man with only the foggiest notion of South Bay geography, and soon the convoy was hopelessly lost, heading for Sunnyvale. I was bringing up the rear in my beat-up, unwashed 1950 Chevy.

Finally the motorcade stopped; we alit from our cars, and the chagrined P.R. man asked, "Does anyone have the faintest idea how to get to Santa Cruz?" As the only person present who knew the terrain, I was instantly elevated to convoy commander. I tooled my inelegant car up to the front, gave a sweep-

ing "follow me" signal, and swung the whole motorcade around in a huge U-turn in midafternoon traffic on The Alameda.

I led the parade all the way to Santa Cruz, with Kefauver and his whole retinue of supporters, aides, flunkies, and lackeys following blindly. By this time the senator was running an hour late, about normal for him. Taking my job as trail boss seriously, I decided the decent thing to do was help him make up some of his lost time. So as we headed out of Los Gatos into the mountains, I hit the accelerator. The speed limit then, as now, was 55 miles per hour (the 65-mph era came in between), but I soon had the whole caravan doing 70. I wondered what I'd say if a cop pulled me over. I decided the last thing I would tell him (after the other cars had sped past) was the truth: "But officer, I was leading a presidential motorcade!" Fortunately no red light appeared in my rearview mirror, and I made up 15 minutes of Kefauver's lost time in getting him over the mountains.

The episode gave me a fleeting sense of power. For one brief hour I had a presidential candidate and his whole campaign totally under my control. I could have taken him so deep into the Santa Cruz mountains, I guess, that he would never have found his way out before the convention.

My first encounter with Caspar Weinberger, who would become President Reagan's secretary of defense, took place in 1954 in Morgan Hill's Live Oak High School. Even then his star had begun to rise.

He was a freshman in the State Assembly at the time, but not a lowly freshman. That was one of his troubles. On reaching Sacramento, Cap had promptly violated the code decreeing that first-termers should be seen but not heard. He had uncorked a liquor license bribery scandal and energetically pursued it in hearings all over the state. The expose had made him an instant political superstar but hardly endeared him to the Legislature's old guard, especially after his disclosures sent the speaker of the Assembly, the late

Charles Lyon, to jail. Another officeholder, the late William Bonelli of the State Board of Equalization, fled to lifetime exile in Mexico.

Cap was a hot drawing card as speaker for the Morgan Hill Republican Assembly that first time I met him in the Live Oak High cafeteria. One of his reasons for being there was to give a boost to his Sacramento officemate, San Jose Assemblyman (now judge) Bruce F. Allen, who was facing a tough re-election campaign. (Like all freshmen, they shared humble quarters in the State Capitol. They were doubled up in an office opposite the elevators, opening on a glorified light well.)

In Sacramento, Weinberger learned the knack of keeping atop the publicity tide. One of his bills, which generated a deluge of mail to every legislator, was aimed at cancer quacks; it would have outlawed their hocus-pocus cures. The quacks mobilized and beat it, though it finally became law in a later session when re-introduced by the late Sen. John F. "Jack" Thompson of San Jose.

From the outset, Cap was a favorite of the State Capitol press corps. He provided lively copy, gave straight answers, and returned reporters' phone calls—habits he took to Washington with him later.

San Jose Mercury News

"Cap" Weinberger as a young assemblyman.

San Jose Mercury News

Bruce Allen (now judge) shared Cap's office.

In the '50s it was not deemed sinful for a legislator to let a lobbyist take him to dinner, and Weinberger enjoyed Sacramento gastronomically. As a member of the San Francisco delegation, he was sometimes entertained by that city's lobbyist, Don Cleary, who at first had trouble sizing him up. But after a few dinners, Cleary said, "I've finally found his weakness. With some legislators it's money; with some it's women; with Cap it's lamb chops."

Weinberger's legislative career lasted three terms before he abandoned it to make a run for state attorney general in 1958. He lost the GOP primary to Congressman Pat Hillings, an intimate friend and confidant of Richard Nixon. Hillings in turn lost in November to Democrat Stanley Mosk, now on the State Supreme Court.

Somewhere among my mementos I have a credential declaring me an honorary assistant sergeant-at-arms of the 1964 Republican National Convention in San Francisco. Several other California political writers of the time, both Republicans and Democrats, have similar certificates, I'm sure. We have Weinberger to thank for them.

They were not bestowed for reasons of honor or ego-stroking, but as emergency gear. By then Cap was chairman of the Republican State Central Committee; it was a time of turmoil within the party, with the radical rightwingers of the John Birch Society trying to seize the reins. By and large they detested the working press, and there were efforts afoot to keep us off the floor of the San Francisco convention, where the conservatives counted on nominating their hero, Barry Goldwater. We feared our news credentials would be little honored.

Weinberger, whom the Birchers despised, was determined that his California press corps, at least, would have maximum access to the floor and the caucus rooms. As state chairman of the party, he had a quota of floor passes to give out. Normally they would have gone to bigwigs and "checkbook Republicans," but Cap issued the sergeant-at-arms passes to the regulars who covered politics for the California media. If our press cards failed us, we could become instant officials of the convention and carry on regardless.

As things turned out, the press was roundly booed, hooted at, and hassled a little by some of the GOP delegates who gathered in the Cow Palace, but generally our regular credentials worked. I, at least, never had to pull rank as a "sergeant-at-arms."

Though the arch-conservatives deemed Weinberger a dangerous liberal in 1964, Ronald Reagan did not share that view when he became governor. He tapped Weinberger for his top executive appointment, state finance director, a post in which Weinberger sharpened the penny-pinching instincts that would earn him the sobriquet "Cap the knife" when he later became Richard Nixon's budget chief in Washington. (Now, as defense secretary, he is thought of as something of a spender.)

Once when Weinberger was state finance director I dropped past his office to find him red-eyed. The state budget, a tome in minute type approximating the size and weight of the San Jose Yellow Pages, was in preparation, and Cap had just finished personally reading galley proofs on the whole book, some 2,000 pages. There wasn't a loose dollar in the budget he didn't know about.

Just as Weinberger once accommodated me with a spurious political credential, I once rescued him in time of distress with a loan of my press card, at the 1968 GOP convention in Miami Beach. The day's proceedings had dragged on interminably; the irritability level in the hall equalled the humidity outside; and all the food at the concessions—junk food at best—had long since given out. I encountered a forlorn Weinberger wandering with his young son in a corridor off the arena. Both were wan and weak from hunger.

The only food left in the building was in the "railroad lounge," a traditional oasis operated at the national conventions by the nation's railroads for reporters only; no delegates admitted. The fare inside was sumptuous: plump sandwiches of juicy roast beef, corned beef, ham, and turkey, served free with sudsy beer and soft drinks.

Taking pity on the future secretary of defense, I slipped him my admission credential, and in the illicit guise of a reporter he stocked up on enough victuals to last him and his son the rest of the session.

CHAPTER IV
Characters

The rhyming doc... the Nobel laureate... the poet laureate... the woman who talked to God... the letter-writing champ... the perennial candidate... Dagobert Ghlue.

With passing time, every reporter attracts his own coterie—his band of loyalists who supply tips, insights, counsel, color for his copy, grist for his mill. They are variously motivated; some by simple friendship, some by an urge to influence directly or vicariously the public dialogue, some by love of the limelight. The reporter cherishes one and all. If he happens to write a column, they become his cast of characters.

In my coterie, none outranks Milton Chatton, a physician long since retired. Each morning at breakfast in his home in old Willow Glen, Chatton peruses the *Mercury* assiduously. Usually he zeroes in on two or three stories—items which illuminate the bizarre flounderings of Mankind, injustice in any form, or especially the bumblings of government bureaucrats.

The latter subject fascinates him because he was once part of the bureaucracy himself, battling its inanities from within. For seven years he was Santa Clara County director of medical institutions, the boss of Valley Medical Center when it was still called County Hospital. He says I was the first San Josean he met when he came as a young doctor to take the job in 1952. Certainly I was the first reporter he met; *News* city editor Dick Barrett sent me out to interview him the day he arrived. Chatton, who until then had done most of his doctoring in an academic setting

at the University of California, confessed to me years later that the interview filled him with terror. He was totally alien to the publicity glare that would surround him as a public official.

I must have broken him in well, for during his time at County Hospital he became a great favorite of the press. He proved one of the most articulate, candid, and fearless of officials in his public utterances.

Not until a quarter-century had passed, however, did I learn that he possessed an additional skill beyond his medical and administrative attainments. He is an accomplished doggerelist. My column readers, over the years, came to know him as "M.C., the rhyming doc."

His breakfast table browsing is central to his creative process. By the end of his second cup of coffee, he will have composed three or four jingles, often limericks—his pithy commentary on the events of the day. I became the beneficiary of his output. His scope is universal; over the years he has expounded in iambic pentameter on everything from cancer quackery to the medfly, everyone from Rose Bird to Idi Amin.

Chatton's classic is probably the verse he dashed off a few years ago in the aftermath of disclosure that Nobel laureates were contributing to a Southern California sperm bank whose clientele was restricted

M.C., the rhyming M.D.

to super-intelligent women. The aim was to propagate a strain of super-humans. Most publicized of the contributors was Stanford's Dr. William Shockley, equally famed as co-inventor of the transistor and propounder of a theory that whites are inherently the intellectual superiors of blacks. After pondering these matters briefly, M.C. dashed off:

Recipients of prizes from Alfred Nobel
Have spermatozoa to donate or sell.
If ladies from Mensa are attractive and willing,
Such impregnation will not cost a shilling;
But if a bright lady turns out to be black,
I'm sure Dr. Shockley will want his sperm back.

Bill Shockley himself joined my cast of characters for a time, providing spice for my readers. A man of gargantuan ego, he relishes the media controversy that swirls about him as much as he relished his appearance before the king of Sweden to accept the 1956 Nobel prize for his transistor work. Interviewing him is like interviewing the Encyclopedia Britannica. Or getting stuck on flypaper.

For me the process began during the Carter-Ford campaign of 1976 when I dialed a number shown on a press release Shockley had issued. He was suggesting that Jimmy Carter take a lie detector test. The first sound I heard was his crisp voice: "Shockley." The second sound I heard was "beep!" Every word the scientist utters into a telephone goes onto tape.

I told him who I was and arranged to interview him the following Tuesday at his home on the Stanford campus. I hung up. Five minutes later my phone rang. This time I heard "beep!" even before "Shockley here." He wanted me to read him the compound decimalized number (like "464.1-minus-2") on the press release before me. He wasn't sure what he had sent out, but he wanted to send me some more literature. I gave him the number and hung up again.

Ninety seconds later my phone rang again: "...(beep!)...Shockley here. I forgot (beep!) to get your address. See you next (beep!) Tuesday. Goodbye!"

A thick packet of additional material was on my desk the next morning, special delivery. It was only the beginning. Among the documents the inventor had sent was a story from the Detroit *News* leading off:

> Prof. William Shockley of Stanford University is one of the most unpopular men in America. Almost everywhere he goes he is called vile names and denied free speech.
> What is so awful about Prof. Shockley? Why do liberal university audiences treat him like Adolf Hitler reincarnated?
> Because (he)...insists that blacks are genetically inferior to whites in terms of I.Q.

On this article Shockley had scribbled, "This is one in which I approved (indeed, wrote) the copy. W.S."

Shockley, wearing sport shirt and slacks, greeted me the following Tuesday at the door of his home and led me down a hall to a sanctum perhaps 11 or 12 feet square. Cluttered bookshelves rose above a cluttered desk. This was several years before the advent of the home computer, but the professor had rigged his own. A super-sophisticated IBM Selectric typewriter was hooked to a "mag card" memory device which stored pages of text that could be retyped automatically at the touch of a button. Like a kid with an electric train, Shockley delighted in showing off the arrangement. He reminded me pointedly, with twinkling eye, that the memory unit was "full of transistors."

"I only learned to type a few years ago," he said. He told me a typewriter had been delivered to the Stanford physics lab during a Vietnam War sit-in there, and he had taken it home. He had been pecking out his own stuff ever since.

The key to our interview turned out to be a row of four-drawer filing cabinets lining one wall of the study. In them Shockley's whole life was documented, indexed, crossfiled, annotated, and decimalized. He had a prefabricated answer to every question I asked. If I said, "Tell me about inventing the transistor," he would rummage through his file drawers, and out would come a monograph, treatise, article, press release, booklet, or clipping answering the question at length. I soon had enough reading matter to fill a briefcase.

Once or twice the scientist could not remember the file number to answer a particular question. He would telephone his wife, who was working at his campus office nearby: "What's the (beep!) number? 376-minus-1432? (beep!) Thanks." Shockley would locate the pertinent document and toss it at me.

"You seem to have a prepared answer for everything," I observed.

"It is *very unlikely* you will produce a question I haven't dealt with," he chuckled.

It is hard to imagine a transistorless world today. Man-on-the-moon might still be science fiction. Without transistorized bugging and taping, there likely would have been no Watergate. The hearing aid, the portable radio, the computer, and stereo would be bulky and primitive. The pocket calculator, solid-state TV, the fuel injection engine, and electronic ignition probably would not exist. It is a testimonial to Shockley's patience that he was able to explain his invention to me, a scientific illiterate, in terms that rang a faint bell from high school physics.

A layman thinks of a crystal as a diamond, a grain of sand, or a chip of quartz. Shockley saw it in terms of its atoms and the arrangement of their electrons. Some atoms had electrons to spare; others had "holes" where electrons were missing. Shockley's great achievement was to put crystals together to create a "valve" that would regulate electron flow, or current.

The transistor was the product of eight years of work by the professor and two of his colleagues, W.H. Brattain and John Bardeen, in the Bell Telephone Laboratories in New York. Shockley's first notebook entry, suggesting the idea, was dated December 29, 1939, but it was not until December 16, 1947, that the first transistor worked in the lab.

"How do you date an invention?" Shockley mused. "...from the first gleam in your eye, or from the time some businessman is willing to put dough in it?"

When the transistor came into being, he told me, it had no name; so Bell Lab sponsored a competition to name it. Among the entries were "amplister" and "transitor." One of Shockley's colleagues came up with the winning name, derived from "transfer resistance."

The professor's main compensation for the invention, which revolutionized electronics and industry and which spawned Silicon Valley, was his one-third share of the $39,000 Nobel prize for it. The patents were held by Bell Lab. The inventor evidenced no regrets about his meager monetary reward, but he clearly savored the recognition that had come to him.

"When a Nobel prize is shared," he told me with transparent vanity, "the names are usually listed alphabetically, but on our citation, my name was first."

I changed the subject and discovered that Shockley's notion about intellectual inferiority of blacks was only one facet of his thinking about "dysgenics," which he defined as "retrogressive evolution through the excessive reproduction of the genetically disadvantaged." His ideas were not only inflammatory *per se*, but he combined a dramatists' flair with a scientist's bluntness when he discussed them. He had written, in one of his treatises:

> I propose as a thinking exercise a voluntary sterilization bonus plan. Bonuses, regardless of sex, race, or welfare status, would depend on the best scientific estimates of hereditary factors and disadvantages such as diabetes, epilepsy, heroin addiction, arthritis, etc. At a rate of $1,000 for each point below 100 I.Q., $30,000 put in trust for 70 I.Q. moron potentially capable of producing 20 children might return $250,000 to taxpayers in reduced costs of mental retardation care....
>
> A feature that might frustrate the plan is that those who are not bright enough to learn of the bonus on their own are the ones most important to reach. The problem of reaching such people...might be solved by paying 10 per cent of the bonus in spot cash. Bounty hunters attracted by getting a cut of the bonus might then persuade low-I.Q., high-bonus types to volunteer.

Notwithstanding Shockley's use of the qualifier "voluntary," such talk was enough to make a lot of folks—black, white, or whatever—nervous. You're arthritic? Get sterilized! Epileptic? Get sterilized! Diabetic? Not too bright? Get sterilized—and make a pot of money. You're too dumb to hear of this offer? A friendly "bounty hunter" will turn you in. Shockley's idea was not softened much by his postscript: "I do not advocate implementation of such a policy, but I do advocate objective inquiry."

"Is the I.Q. test really reliable, though?" I asked him.

"Not entirely," he conceded, "but neither is the clinical thermometer."

San Jose Mercury News

Dr. Shockley: "...(beep!)"

"Dr. Shockley," I challenged, "your expertise is in physics. Have you had any formal education in genetics?"

"You don't need much," he said. "Horse breeders and other people get a feel for it."

Once a reporter writes anything about Shockley that he likes (or perhaps even that he doesn't), he becomes the inventor's pen pal and sounding board. For weeks after my stories about him appeared, bulky packages of additional decimalized press releases and pronouncements kept arriving in my mail, and when my phone would ring, I would often find the professor on the line.

He never announced himself by name, however. He had been impressed by my account of his telephone recording habits, and invariably the first word I would hear (in his voice) was, "Beep!"

A bard of a different stripe than M.C., the rhyming doc, is Charles B. "Gus" Garrigus, California's poet laureate. I knew him, long before he earned that distinction, as a jolly, capable state assemblyman from Fresno County in the 1950s and '60s. His desk in a rear corner of the Assembly floor was next to my press desk, and we exchanged a lot of banter.

Garrigus, the fifth to hold the poet laureate title in California, takes the honor seriously. He works in the tradition of the English poet laureates who produce commemorative verse for all momentous occasions. He has found, however, that matters sometimes go awry.

On Pacheco Pass at Romero Overlook, which affords a panoramic vista of San Luis Dam and Reservoir, a bronze tablet displays a poem Garrigus wrote and read at the dam's groundbreaking in 1962. It was a spectacular occasion, with President Kennedy and Gov. Pat Brown (father of Jerry) jointly pushing a dynamite detonator to set off the first explosive charge. Thousands gathered on a barren Merced County hillside to witness the event. But the open setting played accoustical tricks, as Garrigus vividly recalled almost two decades later. The platform guests, to the rear of the loudspeakers, could scarcely hear each other's speeches.

Garrigus was seated directly behind the president with the late United States Sen. Clair Engle, a feisty ex-D.A. from Tehama County who cultivated a rustic manner for political effect but like Garrigus was a serious Shakespearian scholar.

The verses the poet laureate penned for the occasion were a tribute to the California spirit and tradition, with one couplet harking back to the forty-niners:

When Sutter's golden gleam flashed around
*   the world,*
The hot-eyed hordes poured in from every
*   clime.*

When Garrigus returned to his seat after his reading, Engle congratulated him: "A great poem, Gus. You didn't pull any punches, did you?"

"What do you mean, Senator?"

"You know, Gus, that part about the hot-eyed whores coming from all over the world!"

Reporters learn to recognize certain anonymous telephone voices. Often during the Johnson-Goldwater campaign of 1964, I would pick up my phone to hear, with never so much as an introductory hello, the voice I came to call "the woman who talked to God."

I was covering politics then. Sometime in August, three months before the election, she began demanding that I write a straight-out news story proclaiming Barry Goldwater the winner. She was not asking an analysis, a think-piece, or even an outright prediction, had I been inclined to make one. She would not settle for that. What she demanded (no less) was an unqualified declaration that Goldwater was the president-elect.

"It's only August," I protested. "The campaign hasn't even warmed up yet. How can I write what's going to happen in November?"

San Jose Mercury News

Gus Garrigus: "The hot-eyed hordes poured in..."

"Because God says so. He has told me that Mr. Goldwater is going to win, and I want you to announce it."

"What evidence do you have?"

"Isn't it enough, young man, when God tells you something?"

The woman kept calling back throughout the rest of the campaign, insisting that her revelation be published—not as a revelation, but as settled history.

I never found out who she was, but she must have been disillusioned with God when Lyndon Johnson swamped Goldwater by 16 million votes in the November landslide.

Early on a Monday morning in 1967, with the rest of the *Mercury News* crew, I reported to work for the first time at the papers' gleaming new plant on Ridder Park Drive off Nimitz Freeway. Left behind was the shabby shop downtown, at West Santa Clara and Almaden, from which the newspapers had been published for 25 years.

I had barely located my desk in the virginal new office when the telephone on it, whose number I had not yet learned, rang. As I reached to answer, I fleetingly wondered who my first caller in these strange, sterile surroundings would be. The voice I heard a second later did not surprise me. It was that of Andy

Diaz, announcing his candidacy for some political office. Which office it was I do not recall, and it is irrelevant. For Andy's telephone voice, invariably proclaiming a new candidacy, was a familiar one. It still is.

Andy Diaz is San Jose's Harold Stassen. He never lets an election pass without his hat in the ring. He has announced for city councilman, county supervisor, assemblyman, state senator, United States senator, lieutenant governor, and governor. Often he seeks multiple offices in the same election, appearing on the ballot under one heading while soliciting write-in votes under one or more others. By 1979, by his own count, he had gone after public offices 86 times by election or appointment. That he had never attained one fazed him not in the slightest.

He cited the record: Running for council in 1971, he had polled 968 votes. In subsequent races for the same office, his total had grown to 1,950 in 1973, to 9,012 in 1974, to 9,113 in 1976, and to 33,235 in 1978.

"Every time I lose, I lose with more votes. That's progress," he said.

By this time Diaz had come to savor the "perennial candidate" tag I had once hung on him, and he was claiming a championship; he wondered if the *Guinness Book* had a category for losers.

He also claims a world record for political sign-posting. In each campaign his signs blossom on the Santa Clara County landscape like California poppies. He posts them nocturnally on every phone pole, billboard, and tree—and best of all when possible, atop the signs of rival candidates. In this endeavor he has a special flair; his signs go up in bunches—three, five, 10, or 20 at each site. The effect is overpowering: DIAZ DIAZ DIAZ DIAZ DIAZ everywhere.

Because of Andy's wont to switch races, his signs seldom mention a specific office. They display his surname only in the blackest, boldest capitals the printers and silk screeners can supply. Sometimes there are variations; Andy will order a few thousand VIVA DIAZ signs or (picking up another adjective I applied to him) "LEGENDARY DIAZ."

In his campaigns, Andy is combative and imaginative. Once his opponent (ex-Supervisor Sam Della Maggiore, I think) got a little bonus publicity off the police beat when someone tossed a brick through his headquarters window. Diaz was instantly on the phone to me, inquiring how he might gain comparable exposure; would it help if someone lobbed a brick through *his* window?

Andy, whose vocations have ranged from auto body work to hog farming, uses a refreshing candor in his campaign pronouncements. A classic was his response to a council candidates' questionnaire from the National Women's Political Caucus, which was

Andy Diaz: A legend in his time.   San Jose Mercury News

planning to endorse. Diaz wrote, "In my 20 years of running for office I have never received an endorsement. Other candidates have, and they have been sworn elected officials; then they turn out to be corrupt, dishonest, disloyal bastards. For this reason I will not accept or seek endorsements until I have been elected at least once. I have never accepted a bribe or a dime from anyone to finance my campaigns. I work my ass off."

Diaz agreed, however, to answer the questions the NWPC propounded, the first of which, naturally, was what he thought about the Equal Rights Amendment. His response: "Men must accept women for what they are and love them. I support your rights."

Next the questionnaire inquired, "What have you done to further the status of women?" Andy's answer was rhapsodic: "I have fathered several children. I have loved many women... I have had close contacts. I have always loved women. I treat them with compassion, understanding, and I am honest. I am not a phony. I think women are beautiful. I have seen and loved the naked women. I have fought for social and economic status for women all my life. Even the lesbian women; I have expressed my deep feelings of concern."

A strain of religious fundamentalism has always permeated Diaz' campaign material, as attested in the 1979 council race when he wrote, "I, Andrew Diaz, in the responsible position of being the perennial candidate of San Jose and being a humble instru-

ment in the hands of the Heavenly Father as I am, as we all are to work out His purposes, hereby request that Councilman Al Garza take a leave of absence."

In listing his qualifications, Andy once declared, "I have experienced every logical type of political humiliation, so can only express my feelings as I see fit and leave the rest to the Divine Superior."

In each campaign, Diaz seems to manage to get into a scrape with the law. Far from letting such misadventures devastate him, he capitalizes on them. In 1973 he was indicted for pimping, pandering, and prostitution. Six days later he filed for city council on a legalized-prostitution platform.

In 1977 Diaz was arrested for battery and disturbing the peace after a fist fight. He himself tipped off reporters, and the questioning went like this:

> Reporter: Did they arrest the other guy?
> Diaz: No, just me.
> Q. Who hit whom first?
> A. I hit him first. He has been threatening me for years. He's supposed to be a karate expert, and I'm third degree black belt in karate.
> Q. Did you use karate chops on him?
> A. I used everything on him.
> Q. Who won?
> A. I did, but then the police hit me with a billy club. They gave me a black eye and a sore neck.
> Q. Are you mad at the police?
> A. Oh, no, we were taking out our frustrations. I enjoyed it.

As a result of the fisticuffs, Andy was taken to the County Jail where, he complained, the toilets didn't run and the drinking fountain was plugged up. The only thing that worked, in the holding cell, was the telephone, which he used to call not a relative, not a friend, not a lawyer, but the county registrar of voters—to whom he declared his candidacy for lieutenant governor. He hoped this would impress the guards, he told the press, but it didn't: "When I told them I was Diaz, the perennial candidate, they laughed at me. When I told them I was running for lieutenant governor, they really laughed."

In 1979, while campaigning concurrently for U.S. senator and city councilman, Andy clashed anew with the gendarmes. They arrested him for carrying a loaded firearm while tacking up his signs. He complained to the city ombudsman that the arresting officer had said, "All politicians should be shot." Then, in true form, he issued a press release declaring, "Unorthodox election tactics and politics bring on a rash of tickets from the newer members of the local police. Perhaps it is only these who see Diaz as a threatening revolutionary.'' (In that campaign, however, Andy fostered a revolutionary image by wearing a Castro-style beard and fatigues.)

In campaign announcements, Andy habitually soars off into flights of literary imagery: ''Just as surely as the autumn season brings crisp golden leaves, the San Jose election season brings Andy Diaz.'' But there is invariably a note of rebellion, too, an Andy-against-the-world flavor. His masterpiece may have been his declaration of candidacy in 1969:

> My purpose in writing is to expose my political future and interest in the fourth coming (sic) April elections.
>
> In 1965 I was three minutes late for filing and was disqualified.
>
> In 1966 I was hospitalized for a serious back injury and forced to withdraw.
>
> In 1967 my grandfather, who was one adviser, died of a stroke. Also during this time I lost another adviser who was shot in Guadalajara.
>
> To add to these setbacks, a new one has come about. After my grandfather's death I purchased a herd of hogs from my grandmother. I was in the process of fire insurance when fire swept through the pens. I bought the insurance Wednesday and the fire broke out Thursday morning. The insurance would not be effective until the following day. As a result there will be no claim and a total loss...Total value of the animals was $2,000 plus oats and hay. One small hog survived, which was donated to the Church of God.
>
> Due to this loss I will need financial help. Despite all the hardships and tragedy, I have continued to consider the well-being of my fellow friends, and those of dubious character. And that is why I will run for councilman in April.

That release landed on the desk of Ben Hitt, then city editor of the *Mercury*. Ben, who normally admonished me to ''keep it short,'' passed it to me with a note affixed: ''I've never read better reasons for running for public office. There ought to be some way to run this letter in its entirety.''

San Jose's probable letter-writing champion is Abil Layman. For years he has mass-produced acerbic commentaries, directed to the powers that be. Citizens on the street may never have heard of him, but their councilmen, mayors, supervisors, legislators, and congressmen have. They feel his lash regularly.

''Abil Layman'' is a pseudonym, as are other names he sometimes signs: Knox Little III, Warren Pease, Phare Pleigh, Helen Highwater. Behind all these identities is a one-eyed former Army top sergeant whose real name is Sheldon Bayard and whose chosen retirement career is as a thorn in the side of officialdom. In his 70s, he is a natty dresser who favors tweedy suits accented by a rust-colored beret and the opaque left lens of his spectacles, which obscures an eye that has been sightless for decades because of a cataract.

He chose broadside mailings as his needling medium after some experimentation. ''I used to write letters to the editor,'' he explains, ''but then I found that people who write letters to the editor don't know what they're writing about.''

His unshakable opinions run a broad gamut, as shown by a few excerpts from his epistles to officeholders:

> If I were dictator of Santa Clara Valley, I would disband all the planning commissions and abolish the Status of Women Commission and affirmative action. And I would kick labor unions out of all government, and I would put a big sign at the end of each town with a message, to wit: ''Crime in this city is a criminal offense. Criminals will be locked up in uncomfortable cells and the keys will be given to the people.''

> It takes 13 years to build a nuclear plant in this country but less than five years in Japan... Most of the time is taken up talking—wasted in hearings and stays and lawsuits and yak, yak, yak. HOW DO YOU STOP ALL THIS? Probably you don't, but do you recall from history when WOMEN WERE NOT PERMITTED TO TALK IN PUBLIC?

> LOVE YOUR NEIGHBOR, but don't give him any advice. He can sue you if your advice works against him.

Bayard's unabashed male chauvinism does not diminish his friendly regard for such women in politics as Janet Gray Hayes. ''I like Mrs. Hayes,'' he said mid-way through her mayoral term. ''She's harmless, really, and she's dressing a lot better now.''

Although politics is Bayard's passion, he pales at suggestions that he run for office himself.

''Oh, no,'' he says. ''I'm a Hamiltonian on that. Only the rich and successful should hold public office.''

So why does he keep writing?

''It's an ego trip,'' he confesses. ''I go down to City Hall and Mrs. Hayes says hello to me. It makes me a big shot.''

Bayard's unyielding mind-set and libertarian spirit were nurtured in his formative years in his native South Dakota, where his grandfather Charles H. Sheldon, for whom he is named, was the state's second governor from 1893-97—a Republican as one would expect. Bayard is aghast at the emergence of such latter-day liberals as George McGovern on the South Dakota scene.

"When I was growing up there," he says, "we didn't let Democrats use the sidewalks till afer dark."

He concedes, "I'm a bigot anyway. A long time ago Councilman Al Garza called me a bigot, and I looked it up in the dictionary. It said a bigot is someone who holds an idea and won't give it up. So there's nothing wrong with being a bigot. It's just being loyal to your principles."

In his mid-teens Bayard moved to Los Angeles with his family and as a young man drifted into the hotel business there in the early 1930s. He held jobs up to assistant manager in such hotels as the Arcady, the Gaylord, and the Ambassador. In 1937 he struck out for himself and bought the California House, a flea-bag on L.A.'s grimy East Fifth Street. His clientele, as he describes it, consisted of "working people; they worked each day till they made a dollar" —25 cents for a meal at a nearby greasy spoon, 25 cents for a bottle of wine, and 50 cents for no-frills lodgings at Bayard's flophouse. "No bedding," he specifies, "just a pillow and a mattress and bedbugs in the walls."

Bayard remains a cynic about rehabilitation of the downtrodden.

"I've never seen a real skid row inhabitant get off skid row," he says. "They don't want to get off. They don't want to think."

He became a hotel chain magnate of sorts when he bought three other cheap hostelries in Los Angeles.

"One was in Hollywood near Sunset and Vine," he says. "The girls from Earl Carroll's Vanities stayed there; so it was a sort of whorehouse, but not really."

In retirement four decades later, crusty Sheldon Bayard still derives a fringe benefit from his career as a flophouse landlord, which ultimately gave way to jobs as a real estate salesman ("till I decided they were all liars") and a newspaperman on the old Sunnyvale *Standard*. Two of his early tenants at the California House, who got by for half-price because they shared a bed, were sign painters, the Able brothers. Their name stuck in Bayard's mind, and today with slightly altered spelling ("Abil"), it is the name by which he is better known than by his own.

As for "Layman," he says, "It just popped into my head from nowhere in particular."

One set of characters, with a certain uniqueness as a group, enlivened my column for years.

They included Nate Kearns, who sent me quips purportedly overheard at the Manny's Cellar bar. There was Lucas McEvoy, whose specialty was quirks of the law. Occasionally I would receive a letter with a Honolulu postmark from David Kapiolani, who offered philosophical bits. Lester Keynes contributed colorful vignettes of Santa Clara County history. Comparable items reached me regularly from Paul Appollinaire, Elliott Yost, Bud Sester, Elton Bahm, Bud Doyle, Alvin J. Carr, George C. Kelley Jr., Jack Emm, and C.C. Sitmore. And there were others who fed me items under obvious pen names—notably Leroy Zylks, Cadwallader Kripes, and the prolific Dagobert Ghlue.

This group of readers loved to pick arguments with me. Once when I made a passing reference to President Harding as a "philanderer," Dagobert Ghlue jumped all over me demanding proof. Two old ladies from Los Altos joined in, berating me for besmirching the hallowed memory of Harding, then 55 years in his grave. Sometimes these letter writers would generate heated arguments among themselves. On any issue, if McEvoy was pro, Ghlue was con.

It took me a year or two to discern what was happening, but the truth dawned after I got a tip, purely by chance, about Lucas McEvoy. I began examining

San Jose Mercury News

"Abil Layman": a wicked pen.

his mail carefully and comparing it with other letters from my "regulars" as to the typewriter face, the typing style, the penmanship, and certain peculiarities of the envelope addresses (whether written or typed) and the return addresses. The latter were particularly perplexing and often vague, such as "Route 2, Rural, San Jose."

Finally I discovered the truth: Ghlue, McEvoy, Kapiolani, Appollinaire, Kearns and all the others, including the two old ladies in Los Altos, were the same person. He was a man I knew well, once prominent in San Jose. I never divulged his multiple identities, however, preferring to preserve the goose that was laying my golden eggs.

I was not the exclusive recipient of this gentleman's correspondence. He often contributed in his schizophrenic way to our letters-to-the-editor column. Once when the controversy over admitting women to Rotary, Kiwanis, and other men's clubs was raging, the *Mercury News* carried a dozen or more letters pro and con, examining all facets of the issue. Later I learned that about 10 of these letters, on both sides, were the work of Dagobert Ghlue, signing different aliases. One of them won the papers' Silver Pen Award.

To any columnist, of course, the mail is life blood and oxygen. Knocks are as welcome as boosts. One letter I cherished, addressed not to me but to my editor, read:

> I would like to take this opportunity to let you know just how much I enjoy Harry Farrell's column. As soon as I start enjoying it, I'll do just that. In the meantime I have appealed to the surgeon general for a warning label, to wit: "Reading this column is hazardous to your intelligence."

The paper also once received, clipped to one of my columns whose content I have forgotten, a note reading, "This man is wasting your money. Maybe he could do yard work."

One letter I have saved over the years responded to a bit of satire I once attempted. Some years ago the *Mercury News* undertook a promotion stunt called "Scrounging." The idea was that each Sunday the paper would offer a prize (perhaps it was $50; perhaps only a *Mercury News* T-shirt) to any reader who could produce a specified item of nostalgic trivia, such as a ticket stub from the 1938 Rose Bowl game.

One week the item required was a 78-rpm recording of the Andrews Sisters singing "Rum and Coca-Cola," dating from the 1940s. The reporter who wrote the follow-up story announcing the winner had been born long after that decade, however, and he mistakenly wrote "the Lennon Sisters." This caused quite a flap in the office, evoking embarrassment in some quarters and not inconsiderable mirth among the old-timers.

A correction was printed, but I decided to carry the fun a little further. In what I construed to be a humorous item, I concocted a list of similarly anachronistic discs: Linda Ronstadt singing "Pistol-Packin' Mama," Donny and Marie Osmond singing "Don't Sit Under the Apple Tree With Anyone Else But Me," and Joan Baez singing "Praise the Lord and Pass the Ammunition."

A day or two later, a note on baby blue, flower-adorned stationery arrived:

> Dear Mr. Farrell—
> I think you should be more accurate in your reporting.
> On Thursday I spent four hours going from one record shop to another looking for the records you mentioned by Joan Baez, Linda Ronstadt, and Donny and Marie Osmond, until the man at Village Music told me if they were ever made they were never released.
> I think your error was an imposition on my time, and I don't like it in your newspaper.
>   Sincerely yours,
>   Angela Gomez
> P.S.: Merry Christmas anyway.

For two or three years I used this letter in speeches to illustrate the pitfalls of column-writing. Then, purely by chance, I made a discovery. The handwriting was the give-away.

"Angela Gomez" was yet another identity for my tireless critic Dagobert Ghlue–Nate Kearns–Lucas McEvoy–etc.–etc.

President McKinley (arrow, left) at St. James Park, facing St. James Hotel, 1901. His statue now adorns a nearby spot. The throng fills First Street north of St. John. The hotel, second building on that site to bear the name, was razed in the early 1930s to make room for the post office.

CHAPTER V
Hail To The Chiefs

No American president visiting San Jose should take anything for granted.
We snubbed one, stoned one, and gave one a ticket for speeding.

Since the middle of the 19th century, Santa Clara County has made itself felt in the White House.

Three presidents have lived here, one before, one during, and one after his term. Herbert Hoover entered Stanford in its first freshman class in 1891, organized the first Big Game, graduated in 1895, and came to personify the university. Benjamin Harrison taught constitutional and international law at Stanford in 1894, after he left the White House; he lived in Encina Hall on the campus. Young John Kennedy, fresh out of Harvard, came to Stanford in 1940 to audit a course taught by professor Theodore Kreps. For those concerned with omens, its title was "Introduction to Business and Government." JFK rented a $60-a-month campus cottage from Miss Gertrude Gardiner, former housemother of Roble Hall. During that period he got at least one speeding ticket from old-time traffic cop Ben Hickey.

Pathfinder John C. Fremont, the first presidential candidate of the Republican Party, launched his political career from San Jose, where the California Legislature elected him one of the state's first two U.S. senators, even before statehood was declared. His term coincided with the time the state capital was in San Jose. Fremont proved a better explorer than politician, which may have been an American

tragedy. He lost the 1856 presidential election to James Buchanan, who bumbled the country into the Civil War.

During that war, Abraham Lincoln worried about the quicksilver mines at Almaden, because mercury was a strategic material needed for explosives. Ulysses S. Grant visited San Jose as ex-president in 1879, to be showered with flowers by school children and wined and dined at the Auzerais House, a then-elegant hostelry which stood (until after World War II) on West Santa Clara Street between First and Market, about where the American Savings Building is now. In 1880 the Auzerais House hosted the incumbent president Rutherford B. Hayes. He was dined but not wined; he was a teetotaler. William McKinley gave a speech in St. James Park, on the spot where his statue now stands, four months before he was assassinated in 1901. Theodore Roosevelt planted a redwood tree in Campbell.

Hoover was living on the Stanford campus (in the home which has since become the official residence of university presidents) when the Republicans nominated him in 1928. The custom of the time barred him from attending the party convention; so he accepted the nomination in Stanford Stadium. His

Teddy Roosevelt in San Jose, 1903. Left to right: rancher Charles W. Coe (broad-brimmed hat), Stanford University President David Starr Jordan, Roosevelt, co-publisher J.O. Hayes of the Mercury *and* Herald, *University of California President Benjamin Ide Wheeler (partially hidden by Hayes), and Mayor George D. Worswick.*

campaign and presidency were to inspire a later politician of much different stripe, Sen. Alan Cranston, then a youngster in nearby Los Altos. In her biography of Cranston, his sister Eleanor Fowle gives a vignette of Hoover's triumphal return to Palo Alto after his election:

> A whistle blew and a moment later the train pulled in, jerked to a series of false stops, and came to a halt, letting off an obscuring cloud of white steam.
>
> President Hoover, his rubicund face beaming with delight, appeared at the top of the steps of the last car. The crowd roared. Alan, who had properly gauged the action of the train, dashed to the foot of the steps, smiling, to welcome the president. A policeman raced to grab him by his neck and the seat of his pants, lifted him up, and dumped him unceremoniously outside the circle of welcoming city fathers.
>
> The incident of the delighted president and the boy with a million freckles was shown on newsreels across the country. Alan had begun to show his knack for being in the way of things happening.

My first view of a live president came in 1948 when Harry Truman, fighting for his political life, whistle-

stopped through San Jose on a tour billed as "nonpolitical." What I saw did not leave me in awe of the presidency.

San Jose had not been planned as a stop for Truman, an omission that greatly displeased the late John P. McEnery (father of Mayor Tom), who was the city's "Mr. Democrat" of that time and a Truman loyalist since World War II. He had first met HST when the latter, then a senator, headed up the war-waste probe that set him on the route to the White House. Truman had come through Santa Clara County to inspect Sunnyvale's Joshua Hendy Iron Works (now Westinghouse) and the Kaiser magnesium plant at Permanente.

McEnery, who was a passenger on the Truman Special in 1948, kept lobbying for a San Jose stop but ran into adamant resistance from the president's key staffers, Matt Connolly and Clark Clifford. The train would reach San Jose late at night, they said, and HST needed sleep.

Finally, when the tour reached San Francisco, McEnery decided to bypass official channels. Talking himself past the Secret Service (things were much looser then), he made his way to the presidential suite of the Fairmont Hotel and knocked on the door.

A man and his monument: The 31st President, nearing his 85th birthday, outside the Hoover Library.

Sen. Harry S. Truman, chairing a special committee to probe waste in war production, visits Sunnyvale's Joshua Hendy Iron Works (now Westinghouse), 1943.

Margaret Truman answered. From the bathroom the president called to ask who it was.

"It's Mr. McEnery, Dad."

"Well, he's seen a guy in the bathroom before. Send him in."

Entering the presidential presence, McEnery found Truman in wool underwear, shaving "with a straight razor like your grandfather would use."

McEnery put his plea directly: Why couldn't the president's train, which in about 24 hours would be southbound for Los Angeles, stop in San Jose for just a few minutes?

"How many people can you turn out?" Truman wanted to know.

McEnery promised 1,500.

"I'll stop anyplace for 1,500 people," the president said.

The next night when the train rolled into the San Jose depot, the crowd topped 4,000. On the rear platform, Truman turned to McEnery and said, "You're so conservative you ought to be a Republican."

If the throng expected a political stemwinder, though, it was disappointed. The president settled for a bad pun.

"I'm having a great time in California," he began. "I heard yesterday about a man from Nebraska who was visting in Palo Alto and asked a lady, 'How do I get to *San Josie*?' The lady explained to him that in Spanish, 'J' sounds like 'H,' and it was *San Hosay*. Then she asked him how long he would be in California, and he replied, 'Oh, till Hune or Huly.'"

Probably Truman should have skipped the pun. For although he carried California narrowly the next November, he lost Santa Clara County to Tom Dewey by 11,000 votes.

One of the great ironies of our time is that we will never know whether John F. Kennedy was a great president, merely a good president, or a failure. He was denied enough time to establish his rightful place in history. For his thousand days in the White House, however, he governed with a flair that captured the

San Jose Mercury News

Six days before his election in 1960, John F. Kennedy (arrow) drew a crowd of 20,000 that overflowed the San Jose Civic Auditorium parking lot, now the site of McCabe Hall. The camera points southwest toward a bar and drive-in (upper left of center) where the San Jose Public Library stands today.

nation's heart and buoyed its spirit. And the circumstances of his death have made him a larger-than-life figure in our minds. Forgotten today is the astounding speed of his rise.

Late in 1959, Kennedy was in San Francisco as speaker for a $100-a-plate dinner for Northern California Democrats at the Fairmont. I went up to cover it and arrived at the hotel in early afternoon to pick up an advance copy of the senator's text. In the lobby, some 15 or 20 feet inside the main door, I encountered Kennedy talking to his press secretary, Pierre Salinger, my old friend from the California political wars. I joined them, and the three of us conversed for several minutes—small talk as I recall—before we headed for the elevators, I to go to a press room on the mezzanine and Kennedy to his suite.

The lobby was bustling at mid-day, but passersby scarcely gave us a second look. Incredible as it now seems, at that point John F. Kennedy could stand in a crowd in near-anonymity. One year later he was elected president of the United States.

Lyndon B. Johnson's only political visit to San Jose, during his vice presidential term, was a fiasco of such dimensions as to sour him on our town for life.

He came in the fall of 1962, stumping for Don Edwards in his first run for Congress and the rest of the local Democratic ticket. In that era no vice president was a big drawing card, least of all Johnson in California; he lacked the charisma that could get to the hearts of the state's liberals and Kennedy zealots. Moreover, the timing of LBJ's San Jose appearance was ill-conceived and the advance work deplorable. For his main speech a bunting-draped platform had been set up near the front door of City Hall on Mission Street. The vice president was due in late afternoon, 4:30 or 5 o'clock, just when everyone in the Civic Center was getting off work and heading impatiently homeward.

Johnson arrived to find, almost literally, more dignitaries on the platform than voters out front. Even the pitiful turnout of 200 or 300 had been rigged at the last minute by Mayor Robert Welch. Welch was a Republican but nonetheless felt San Jose should produce a half-way decent crowd for the vice president of the United States, if only for appearance's sake. He stalked through the City Hall flushing out secretaries, bureaucrats, draftsmen, engineers—anyone he could find to inflate the audience.

Alas, the effort was insufficient to sooth the terrible-tempered LBJ. He seethed through his prepared remarks and then berated the local Democratic hierarchy all the way to the Hyatt House where a VIP reception awaited him.

He never visited San Jose again.

By the time he was president, Richard Nixon knew Santa Clara County well, having stumped it often in his senatorial, gubernatorial, and presidential campaigns. He chose Santa Clara's Buck Shaw Stadium for the first full-scale rally of his bid for the White House in 1968. Two years later, San Jose would produce one of the most violent episodes of his presidency.

He came here on October 29, 1970, six days before that year's congressional election, trying to shore up the Republican campaign, notably the faltering re-election effort of Sen. George Murphy (who would lose to Democrat John V. Tunney the following Tuesday).

Nixon was in San Jose only an hour and 35 minutes, but what happened between the landing and takeoff of Air Force One at Municipal Airport colored the rest of the campaign throughout the land.

The Vietnam fighting was still heavy then, with protest running high. Plans for a demonstration against the president were announced beforehand in fliers circulated at San Jose State and elsewhere, signed by five groups—the San Jose Liberation Front, the Radical Action Movement, the Revolutionary Union, the Santa Clara County Workers Committee, and the Peace and Freedom Party. Separate plans for peaceful picketing were announced by a group of unemployed hard-hats. Some 2,000 shouting peace marchers greeted the Nixon motorcade when it rolled into the Civic Auditorium parking lot (where the San Jose Convention Center is now) about 7 o'clock in the evening.

Inside the hall, Nixon found a cheering audience of Republicans, including then-Gov. Ronald Reagan. His speech had one hard kernel of news, a flat denial of assertions by Tunney that the government planned to close NASA's Ames Laboratory.

What happened as the president left, he relates in his memoirs:

> As I walked the few steps to my car after the speech, I could see the protesters gathered on the other side of the police barricades just a hundred feet away. They were chanting their favorite slogans, including, "One, two, three, four—we don't like your fucking war," and I could not resist showing them how little respect I had for their juvenile and mindless ranting. I stood on the hood of my car and gave them the V-sign that had become my political trademark. It had a predictable effect, and a chorus of jeers and boos began. Then I saw something coming toward me. When it hit the roof of the car, I realized that it was a rock. Suddenly rocks and eggs and vegetables were flying everywhere. Within seconds I was in the car, and Secret Service agents were following emergency evacuation procedures. Unfor-

tunately one of the cars in the motorcade behind us stalled, and its windows and windows in the press bus were broken by rocks. Several people, including Secret Service agents, were hit by rocks and flying glass.

Later there would be deep partisan suspicions about the happenings that evening. Democrats would question whether the hostility had been inspired, or at least condoned, by the Republicans as a sympathy ploy. Nixon was quick to make political capital of it; in a speech two days later in Phoenix he branded the San Jose demonstrators as "the same thugs and hoodlums that have always plagued the good people." Some Democrats would assert that the president distorted the facts, that he was never in danger.

Nixon was right, at any rate, about the press bus. I was on it, and missiles pelted the window beside me. The windshield was shattered. One thing still puzzles me though: how the Secret Service ever let the presidential caravan get surrounded in the first place.

San Jose Mercury News

LBJ smiled for the camera, but he was fuming inside; Mayor Robert Welch at right.

It took a flying wedge of white-helmeted San Jose police to open a route through the crowd for the trapped cars.

Eleven years later, in 1981, a haunting echo of the San Jose strife turned up cryptically on a pre-Watergate White House tape obtained by the New York *Times*. It had been recorded May 6, 1971, six months after the San Jose incident. On it were the voices of Nixon and his chief of staff, Bob Haldeman, considering how to deal with a peace march then in progress in Washington. Nixon instructed Haldeman:

> So therefore, play it hard. Play it responsibly but play it hard and don't back off from it. Now they can—you see, they'll all think back to the San Jose thing, and forgetting that San Jose was fine except for the goddamned silly speech, you know. Covering that getaway from it; we got (unintelligible) home free. We had it all on our side.

It was a different, happier memory of San Jose that Nixon summoned up when I visited him at San Clemente in the summer of 1978, four years after he resigned the presidency. He was just emerging from his recluse period; I was the fifth or sixth reporter to get a one-on-one interview with him. (David Frost paid $600,000 for the first; I got mine free.)

Our conversation ranged widely for 20 minutes or so. As it drew to a close, well into the lunch hour, Nixon harked back nostalgically to his 1950 campaign for senator.

"Does San Jose still have that great restaurant," he asked, "...the one where you could buy ice cream and candy, too?"

It took me a minute to think of the long-gone place he meant.

"O'Brien's?"

"O'Brien's!" he exclaimed. "That's right, that was one of the best restaurants in California."

On that note our visit ended.

Gerald Ford was the only recent president to spend the night in San Jose while in office. He came through for a couple of speeches in 1976 and stayed at the downtown Holiday Inn.

After he left, Charli Kopp got to poking around in his suite and made a startling discovery: the bathroom door was weird, capable of being locked only from the *outside*.

"If the president of the United States can be locked

San Jose Mercury News

At Municipal Airport after the stoning, October 29, 1970. From left: the author, U.S. Sen. George Murphy, President Nixon.

in the bathroom," she said, reporting her find, "one wonders who's running the country."

As vice president in 1974, Ford detoured to San Jose from a Pebble Beach golfing visit to address the Republican State Central Committee and help re-elect Congressman Pete McCloskey, and his luck was scarcely better than Johnson's had been.

Raising a crowd was not his problem; several hundred GOP committeemen provided a ready-made one. But they were in a surly mood, for arrangements had gone awry at the then brand-new Le Baron Hotel, where the meeting was held. The untested Le Baron crew had oversold the house by some 300 rooms, and delegates with confirmed reservations had ended up in third-rate motels as far away as Sunnyvale.

Moreover, with the press clamoring for a Ford news conference, the hotel could not even supply a proper meeting room and lectern. The vice president of the United States ended up fielding reporters' questions in the dim light of an intimate cocktail lounge.

Ford did not turn off on San Jose as Johnson did, however. He later invested in it, acquiring an interest in the Garden Alameda office complex. At least San Jose treated him better than Sacramento and San Francisco did. There, they tried to shoot him.

Ronald Reagan was still a Democrat when he paid his first political visit to San Jose (perhaps his first visit ever) in 1961. But he was the sort of Democrat, by then, who was welcomed by Republicans as speaker for their annual $100-a-plate dinner. In the early 1960s he was still hosting the *General Electric Theater* and touring the land under the General Electric aegis preaching capitalism and anti-communism.

In those days Reagan refused to fly. His GOP hosts had to schedule him early, hustle him out of the hall (at Lou's Village), and rush him to the depot so he could catch the "Lark" home to Los Angeles. Within a few years he was back in town as a Republican by registration as well as inclination, testing the gubernatorial waters. He would tap our town for some of the top talent of his governorship and presidency. Lyn Nofziger, Reagan's off-and-on press secretary both in Sacramento and on the presidential campaign trail, learned his journalism at San Jose State. Mike Deaver, one of the awesome "big three" on Reagan's White House staff, started in politics as the one-man staff of the Santa Clara County Republican Central Committee. The job didn't pay much; so Mike moon-

As minority leader of the House of Representatives, a slim Gerald Ford visited San Jose in 1967 to speak at a $100-a-plate Republican dinner. With him are Mrs. Herbert Fisher and ex-Congressman Charles S. Gubser.

lighted as a piano player at the Interlude bar at Third and Santa Clara Streets.

During a courtesy call Reagan paid as governor on *Mercury News* publisher Joe Ridder, he demonstrated that the presidency, which he had coveted since at least 1968, did not especially awe him.

The conversation ran to small talk, and Joe told a tale about Richard Nixon, then new in the White House. For some reason long forgotten, Nixon had been trying to reach Ridder by phone. The White House had called the newspapers' switchboard, but our operator had orders not to give out the publisher's home number. She put the White House on "hold" while she called Ridder at home and asked if she could break the rule. Joe replied, "Of course," of course.

Regaling Reagan with the story, he said, "Can you imagine being asked whether it was all right to put the president through?"

Reagan cogitated for a moment before responding mischievously, "Well, it would have been sort of fun to say no."

San Jose Mercury News

Hard-hatted sportswriter Dan Hruby edits the last story in the old Mercury News *plant downtown, February 5, 1967.*

CHAPTER VI
From Deadline To Deadline

San Jose's pulse is best felt in its newsrooms. Over the decades the quarters have gone from businesslike to barnlike and back again, but the writers have always laughed a lot.

One thing the *Mercury News* lost when it moved in 1967 from its battered downtown building to its moat-enclosed palace off Nimitz Freeway was its endless stream of walk-in people: tramps, loudmouthed lawyers, showbiz characters, musclebound jocks, panhandlers, fancy ladies, pugnacious politicians, evangelists, growers of 40-pound squashes, visionaries, inventors, cross-country joggers and bikers.

Some of these types still come to see us at our stately home "in the country," but not on impulse anymore. At the old shop, a few steps took them from the Almaden Avenue sidewalk into the newsroom, and they all brought their stories—even the irate litigants from the divorce or criminal courts who, feeling wronged in print, were looking for an editor to punch in the nose.

This passing parade sometimes caused confusion, as when Wayne Danielson, a cub reporter of the 1950s who has become an eminent journalism professor, wondered about a handsome gent who strode past his desk several times. Told it was the publisher, Joe Ridder, Danielson said, "I thought he was a cowboy actor."

For much of my stay in the downtown plant, my desk was so situated that I intercepted the stream of humanity coming through the door. Senators, governors, and would-be presidents were part of the stream. Pat Brown came, and Ronald Reagan.

William F. Knowland, minority leader of the U.S. Senate, cooled his heels outside the editor's office awaiting an interview he hoped would produce an endorsement. Gov. Goodwin J. "Goodie" Knight would plop himself down in a chair beside my desk and tell stories for half an hour.

Among the most disreputable-looking visitors was an old man wearing a crumpled, sweat-stained hat, uncreased pants, and a four-day stubble of beard, who shuffled past me one day and began rummaging through the nearby desk of columnist Frank Freeman. Who's this bum, I wondered? I went over to challenge him.

"Hey, you, what the hell do you think you're doing?" I asked.

"Frank said he'd leave a paper here for me."

Still unsatisfied, I demanded some I.D.

"I'm Charlie Lockwood," the interloper said.

Then I recognized him. I had been about to give the heave-ho to the admiral who had commanded the whole Pacific submarine fleet, under Nimitz, in World War II.

Until 1942 the *Mercury Herald*, as it was then called, and the *News* were separately owned. The former was published from a prosperous-looking plant on West Santa Clara Street just off First Street, now a part of the Bank of the West Building.

The deadline nears for the last edition of the Mercury News *published downtown, February 5, 1967.*

The latter was a feisty, struggling competitor issued from a store-front office on West San Antonio Street (now the Paseo de San Antonio). But the relative opulence of the *Mercury* was illusory because the papers, competing in a town of about 75,000 in the wake of a 13-year depression, were in danger of going under. A series of changes during one hectic year saved them.

First the *Mercury* gave up its impressive, costly-to-maintain quarters adjoining the city's main crossroads and moved three blocks west into the low-rent district. The new plant had been what passed for a supermarket in the 1930s. It was a cavernous barn that brought every department of the paper, from the switchboard and the cashier's cage up front to the presses in the rear, into a single room. Not even the publishers, Elystus and Harold Hayes, had private offices. Departments were separated by railings no more than four feet high, and when the presses rolled, the undamped roar reverberated through the whole building. Signs of the structure's former use were everywhere: part of the butcher department's tile floor was still visible in the composing room. (To this day, the name "California Public Market" can be read through peeling paint on the rear of the building.)

Some face-saving explanation for such crude accommodations (other than tough times) had to be given the public; so the set-up was touted as a model of horizontal efficiency allowing the business of the newspaper to flow unimpeded from the front door to the presses. It was not long, however, before this rationale was dropped, and a vast glass partition was installed from floor to ceiling, about half-way back, to shield the business and editorial departments from the clatter and thunder of the back shop.

As time passed and prosperity returned, this Spartan plant would be repeatedly remodeled and expanded to occupy the whole block on the north side of West Santa Clara Street between Almaden and Notre Dame. Finally, an addition was built for the presses on the Notre Dame side, and some cosmetic work was done to the exterior, unifying the hodgepodge of old and new structures into a reasonable facsimile of a modern building. It still stands at this writing, with a "To Lease" sign hanging forlornly in the window.

The second turning point of 1942 came in late summer after nerve-wracking weeks of rumors that either or both of the San Jose papers might imminently fold. The *Mercury* bought the *News.*

As finally consummated, the deal had a hocus-pocus, flimflam flavor, because it was unveiled in two stages, the second stage dumfounding some of those with the most at stake, namely the *News* staff. The Payne family, which had owned the paper since the 1920s, wanted to unload it, but the word was they would never sell to the detested *Mercury.* The first announcement of the sale, appearing in the *News*, named the buyer as one Smith Davis, about whom little was known. Three or four days later he turned out to be a newspaper broker from the Midwest, who was fronting for the Hayes family, the *Mercury* owners. San Jose's era of cutthroat daily newspaper competition was over.

By sheer coincidence, I arrived at the *Mercury* office the same day the *News* did. On September 1, 1942, the first day both papers were edited from the same shop, I came aboard as the copyboy. I say *the* copyboy because there was only one for the whole establishment—all departments—and today's more genteel title "copy clerk" had not been coined.

I worked the swing shift, from 3 to midnight, and there was hardly any part of the operation I didn't have a hand in. Running copy from the city editor's wire basket to the composing room (rather the composing area, because it was all one room) was but a small part of the job. For my $17.50 a week, my duties also included going to the post office four times a shift for the mail and distributing it; putting out the Saturday church page; buying pipe tobacco (Revelation) for city editor Bob Ryan; picking up the syndicate mats and the Sacramento Bureau copy at the old bus station on South Market Street; obtaining the final stock list (then severely abbreviated) from E.F. Hutton and copying the numbers onto galley proofs to be set for the morning edition; reading the rain

Until 1942, the Mercury *emanated from this building at 30 West Santa Clara Street. Remodeled, it is now the west wing of the Bank of the West.*

gauge on the roof of the office; cranking open the ceiling windows in the back shop; copying the day's marriage licenses at the county clerk's office and visiting the city and county health departments for the births; and compiling the "San Jose Today" column, which included the vital statistics, divorces, sun, moon, and tide reports from the Coast and Geodetic Survey, building permits, and daily butter, egg, and poultry quotations.

The foregoing duties amounted to about half the job. I also prepared the index for page one; compiled the theater time table (which wasn't too hard because there were only nine movie houses in the city); manned the switchboard during the regular operator's break; purchased the papers' postage stamps (for cash) at the post office; changed typewriter ribbons for the whole staff; packaged and mailed out mats of a religious column written by a long-dead member of the Hayes family but still syndicated weekly to the Monterey *Peninsula Herald* and San Bernardino *Sun*; performed a similar chore for garden editor Rolly Langley, who syndicated his column to the Oakland *Tribune*; purchased the late edition of the San Francisco *Call-Bulletin* and the overnight editions of the *Examiner* and *Chronicle* from the crippled newsboy at First and Santa Clara; and saw that every paste pot in the office was filled.

Since I was still going to school, they told me considerately that I could do homework in my *spare* time.

Of all the duties I have listed, the most distasteful

The Mercury News *moved into the central section of this plant, a converted grocery store at 211 West Santa Clara Street, in 1942. It eventually expanded to occupy the full block before moving to Ridder Park Drive in 1967.*

beyond doubt was filling the paste pots. The reeking barrel of sour flour paste, kept in the circulation shed at the extreme rear of the building, served as home for a swarm of voracious gnats; I had to fight them off as I filled the pots, using a wooden ladle big enough to paddle a canoe with.

Still, the job was seventh heaven for a teenager fresh from the staff of the San Jose High School *Herald* who was intent on becoming a professional journalist. Close reading of the foregoing job description will disclose that while I wrote a lot of copy for the newspaper, it was all statistical or tabular material—generally speaking, all set in eye-straining 5½-point type, in those days called "agate." Under the Guild contract, the copyboy was forbidden to do anything in the slightest way creative; that had to be done by a reporter, whose pay scale started at something like $25 a week. This restriction was frustrating to me, for I was itching to try my hand at a real news story.

My chance finally came, and I persuaded Steve Murdock, the City Hall reporter and president of the Guild, to let me cheat on the contract a little. The city health department, where I picked up the births, issued a weekly communicable disease report, and Steve said I could write it up in story form if I wanted to.

In a typical week, the report showed half-a-dozen cases each of measles, mumps, whooping cough, and chickenpox, one or two of scarlet fever and salmonella, and in a bad week, perhaps a case of polio. It was not very exciting stuff. I saw an opportunity for creativity, however, one week when two cases of syphilis were reported. In the comparable week a year earlier, there had been only one. I was elated when I somehow got a story past the copy desk and into the paper with a gee-whiz lead reading something like, "Syphilis has doubled in San Jose during the past year, City Health Officer Dwight M. Bissell reported today." Looking back today on this early excursion into yellow journalism, I still find great satisfaction in my youthful ingenuity.

I must digress here for a further word about Steve Murdock. His desk was next to mine in the office, and he spent hours teaching me the craftsmanship of the reporter, how to combine the elements of a complex situation rapidly into a well-constructed piece of copy. I still do many things much the way he taught me.

In all these sessions, he never tried to indoctrinate me politically, which was just as well, for Steve was in fact what many newswriters of the time were falsely accused of being—a professing, practicing, and dedicated Communist. He would later become editor of

the *People's World*, the West Coast counterpart of the *Daily Worker*.

When I returned to the *News* as a cub reporter after my stint in the army during World War II, I took over Steve's old beat, City Hall. It was pretty much a conservative enclave then, but I found that everyone had a good word for Steve. Time after time I was told that if I could report half as fully, accurately, and fairly as he had, I'd do all right.

Many years later, when I was covering state politics, I would often run into Steve. Representing the *People's World*, he showed up at many statewide Democratic meetings; it was probably true that the Communists were trying to plant their party line in the Democratic platform. Sometimes on these occasions, if I happened to miss a press conference or similar event, I would seek out Steve for a "fill." I never had the slightest qualm about doing so. For his own paper, I'm sure, he slanted the story to the party line, but when he briefed me, he was scrupulously accurate, thorough, balanced, and fair.

Steve Murdock was a Communist with integrity.

From the day the *Mercury* and *News* merged, the cry of "monopoly press' has been heard in San Jose. It has been largely a spurious alarm, for San Joseans have never had to rely on a single source for news of their community. In recent times the two papers have become substantially a unified operation to compete with television, radio, the suburban weeklies and the San Francisco dailies. But for the first 10 years after the merger, as long as the Hayeses remained as publishers, the *Mercury* and *News* editorial staffs stayed totally separate. We cooperated only on the Sunday paper; throughout the week, the inter-staff competition was unabated.

Working out of one city room caused some problems for the dual staffs but also afforded some opportunities. We shared the same desks—battered old typewriter desks of solid oak, bearing the scars of long service and the burns of countless cigarettes. Each desk had three drawers. As the *News'* City Hall man, I was supposed to have one drawer as my inviolate personal space; another belonged to my *Mercury* counterpart; the third was a common area for storing copy paper and supplies. After a time, I began to suspect that the *Mercury's* man was snooping in my drawer, riffling through my notes to find out what I was working on. I decided to set him up.

I concocted out of whole cloth a story that was ludicrous but plausible, and I fabricated a lot of notes and memos to myself, both hand-written and typed, concerning it. I think they gave the impression that the City Hall had been condemned and that the Sainte Claire Hotel, then the city's finest, was to be

San Jose Mercury News
Patricia Loomis: Scooped on her own crusade.

commandeered as a replacement. I left these notes carelessly exposed in my own drawer. My *Mercury* rival took the bait. I immensely enjoyed the feedback I got on the beat, where he was asking questions for days trying to confirm my spurious yarn.

The competition between *Mercury* and *News*, which continued after the merger, was fostered by the rival city editors and encouraged by top management. A reporter who lost a story to the opposition had some explaining to do to his city desk. On one memorable occasion, however, *News* city editor Dick Barrett reacted with unruffled, philosophical kindness when one of his young reporters, Patricia Loomis, was scooped on her own beat. Pat was covering the San Jose schools in the late 1940s, at a time when an inept superintendent was heading for trouble. Her aggressive reporting of his bungling had led the school board almost to the point of firing him. So when he finally submitted a face-saving resignation, he broke the story to her *Mercury* rival, whom I'll call Gladys, because that's about as far from her real name as one can get. The superintendent had always favored Gladys, and with good reason; she wrote everything just the way he told her to.

Pat was heartbroken and furious to be beaten on the payoff of her own crusade. To Barrett she wailed, "How could Gladys get ahead of me on this?" Dick,

rather than upbraid her, just yawned and said, "Oh, the superintendent probably rolled over in bed and said, 'By the way, Gladys, I'm resigning today.'"

A big change in the newspaper business came in the 1930s when unionism gained a foothold in the editorial offices with the advent of Heywood Broun's American Newspaper Guild, CIO. The *Mercury* staff entered the movement early. The Guild was well established when I went to work in 1942. The local charter dates from 1937.

Today the Guild is a highly sophisticated union well staffed with professionals, but in the early days it was a ragtag, do-it-yourself outfit. I was president of the San Jose local in 1951, during the publishing regime of the Hayes family. Co-publishers Elystus "Dit" Hayes and Harold Hayes were first cousins, both gentlemen of the old school but as different as summer and winter. Dit was an attorney, nothing if not dignified, with a fine sense of fair play. He would have made an admirable judge. He was, in fact, a close friend of Chief Justice-to-be Earl Warren; they had been young lawyers together. Harold, by contrast, was a hail-fellow-well-met, who enjoyed nothing more than a belt with the boys at the El Capitan Bar of the DeAnza Hotel, across the street from the paper. He was warm, sympathetic, and a soft touch.

During my term as Guild president, I shamelessly exploited the opposite characteristics of the co-publishers in my grievance strategy. If the facts of a case—whether it concerned a firing, a pay question, an overtime dispute, or a matter of employees' rights—were clearly on the Guild's side, I'd take it to Dit. His passion for justice was so pervasive that he would concede the issue at once when he recognized the rectitude of our position. If on the other hand we were on shaky ground or clearly wrong, I'd go to Harold. We'd give him a pathetic song and dance about our member who had come to work drunk, or deserted his post, or cheated on his expense account, or embezzled the company's funds, or committed a horrendous libel. We'd tell Harold the trouble the fellow was having with his wife or about his small kids, and how contrite the man was. A little of this went a long way, and before the discussion got far Harold would say, "Let's give the poor wretch one more chance."

Using such tactics, I won every grievance that arose during my presidency, except one with a unique twist. At that time, postwar newsprint demand still exceeded supply, and to firm up its supply, the *Mercury News* had tried an end run; it had put a scion of a major newsprint manufacturer on its payroll. This young man could have had a plush job in the executive suite of the family company, but he had an

San Jose Mercury News

Publishers Harold Hayes, left, and Elystus "Dit" Hayes visit the Mercury News *copy desk, as visitors file past during a 1950 open house. The shirt-sleeved deskman with his back to the camera is the late John Moynihan, father of U.S. Sen. Daniel Patrick Moynihan, D-N.Y.*

admirable yearning to make it on his own in the real world, as a newspaper reporter. The problem was, his patrician background had generated little respect in him for the principles of the Guild contract by which he was bound. One clause of the contract said that except under tightly limited conditions, a reporter could not double as a photographer or vice versa.

To the son of the newsprint maker, whom I'll call Clarence, this restriction was intolerable nonsense. He considered himself a photographer *par excellence* and insisted on taking his camera along on every story he covered. Some of his pictures showed up in the paper, and there was hell to pay in the darkroom. The photographers filed an angry complaint that a reporter was illegally usurping their work.

The case ended up in a tense session around a grievance table, with Dit Hayes and a crew of executives on one side and me and my grievance committee on the other. For a half-hour we went round and round, dissecting the somewhat tortured wording of the contract provision that banned reporter-photographer combinations. The whole clause outraged Ken Conn, the old-school executive editor who had come up through the ranks. To him, it was an unconscionable encroachment on journalistic initiative and enterprise. Our Guild position, of course, was that the contract had to be enforced and retreat was out of the question. The argument waxed hotter until Dit, who had been saying little, finally cut through the impasse. He was smiling slightly.

"Look," he said, "let's all be honest. "We're not trying to break down your contract, and we're not trying to set a precedent. But let's face it, Clarence is a prima donna, and if we don't let him take pictures, he may quit. And the Guild doesn't want us to lose our newsprint—does it?"

Everyone around the table started laughing. Dit's word was as good as his bond, and for the Guild we happily threw in the towel. We clued in the regular photographers, and for the rest of the time Clarence was with us, they let him dart around snapping pictures of fender-bender accidents and whatever else caught his fancy.

A few made the paper, but very few. All concerned agreed that work of his caliber would never pose a threat to the job security of the regular cameramen.

The heart of every great newsroom is its rewrite bank, a bunch of professionals who can turn out copy at a thousand words an hour, shaping notes dictated by outside "leg men" into clean, readable prose. Lucky indeed is the beat reporter who is referred by the city desk to a rewrite person with whom he has good rapport. Transformation of a reporter's spoken words into tight, hard copy is not the simple, mechanical process it might seem. It is the subtle melding of the complementary skills of two journalistic specialists, one on the front lines and one at headquarters. Between beat reporter and "rewrite" there is inevitably creative tension, as they haggle over both facts and style.

Mercury reporter Cliff McLean, doubling as a *Chronicle* stringer in the 1940s, regularly phoned his stuff to a woman on the *Chronicle* desk who delighted in posing questions he couldn't answer. So when a grisly wife-murder took place in San Jose, he was determined to have every fact at his fingertips before he called. Besides the obvious—names, addresses, ages, weapons, etc.—Cliff ascertained the color of the victim's hair and eyes, her scars, her history. He got comment from the cops, the coroner, and the neighbors. He was sure he couldn't be stumped as he told how the husband went after his mate with a hammer and then, after beating her brains out, stomped on her with heavy boots. But when he was finished, the *Chronicle* woman demanded, "What was the husband's motive?"

At that point, not even the police had the faintest idea why the man had done it, and Cliff was about to answer, "I don't know." But inspiration struck. Instead, he paused momentarily for effect and then intoned, "I think he was mad at her."

For years, the most onerous rewrite chore on the *News* was the weekly criminal calendar from the

Superior Court. From a dozen to 25 defendants would be on the docket for sentencing, and the story always broke close to the noon deadline. Ordinarily a paragraph was written on each case, as: "Joe Jones, 32, unemployed laborer of such-and-such address, was sentenced to two years in state prison for assault. He had pleaded guilty to the stabbing of Richard Roe, 30, in a Santa Clara tavern brawl."

What made the criminal calendar irksome for the rewrite staffer who got stuck with it was that the lion's share of the work was done in the office. All that the veteran courthouse reporter, Phil Watson, had to do was read off the name and disposition of each case. It fell to rewrite to supply the rest of the facts from the clips in the library.

On one memorable occasion, the criminal calendar wound up early, and Watson could have come in and written his own story. He *did* come in, in fact, but instead of going to his own desk, he picked up an obscure phone in a far corner of the newsroom and dialed rewrite as if calling from the courthouse. His call was given to Jeannette Befame, and he rattled off his rapid-fire notes to her and hung up.

As Jeannette began shuffling through dozens of clippings, trying to match up the background facts with the sentences meted out, Phil walked past her desk with a cheery "Hi, Jeannette," and kept on going out the door on his way to lunch.

Only then did Befame realize she had been stuck with the worst assignment of the week by a colleague sitting 30 feet away, who could have done it himself.

Newsroom characters come and go, and one who enlivened the *Mercury* staff about 30 years ago was the late Milt Phinney. A droll, charming fellow, he brought to San Jose the flavor of the old tabloid journalism. Milt, who covered City Hall for the *Mercury* for a time, had been city editor of the Los Angeles *Daily News* in its prime, and from that harum-scarum rag he imported the philosophy that in the news columns, fun should take precedence over fact. Actually he was a master craftsman when it came to combining hard fact with easy reading. The lead I best remember him for, on an otherwise dry story about a rezoning that involved Rosicrucian Park, was, "A little bit of Egypt fell from out the sky one day—on the block bounded by Park, Naglee, Chapman, and Randol."

Milt was not above embroidering the facts a little to improve readability. His favorite aphorism was, "Never let a fact stand in the way of a good story," with its corollary, "Don't check out your facts too far, or you may prove them wrong."

(The latter rule, incidentally, is not so facetious as it might seem. Once when covering City Hall I was tipped by an unimpeachable but unidentifiable source, City Manager O.W. "Hump" Campbell, to a bribe that had been offered in a Willow Glen rezoning hassle. There was no doubt about it. But by the time I was through questioning all concerned, the culprits had covered their tracks and my proof had vanished. I lost the story—though I had the satisfaction of nipping the skulduggery in the bud.)

Phinney was a consummate raconteur, whose best yarn dealt with events in the L.A. *Daily News* city room. There had been a staff reorganization, with the former movie critic promoted to assistant city editor. Alas, his first weekend alone on the desk was that of December 7, 1941.

When the reports from Pearl Harbor began pouring in, a breathless reporter who had heard them on the radio phoned the office and said, "I guess you'll want the staff to come in on overtime, huh?"

The erstwhile critic yawned and replied, "No, I don't see any local angle to the story."

The next week he was back on the movie beat.

It has been years since I have heard anyone call our newsroom library "the morgue." Thirty or 40 years ago, that's all it was ever called, because it was the place where dead news was interred in the clipping files. But the universal urge for dignity that has converted "dogcatchers" to "animal control officers" and "janitors" to "custodians" has caught up with the news business, too. It is no longer "the morgue;" always "the library" nowadays.

The upgraded nomenclature is deserved, however. Our library has become a complex and sophisticated place, with the old files on microfilm and microfiche, and wondrous optical machines that produce instant print-outs. We even use the Dewey decimal system and a card catalog to keep track of books, reports, and documents.

In the "morgue" days, clips were filed according to the whim of the librarian. Some thought his filing system was his job insurance, since no one else could locate anything. Mao Tse-tung could be found under "T"—for "Tung," naturally. Once when an editor called for mug shot of Stokely Carmichael, he got one of Hoagy Carmichael. When a Scottish woman I'll call Mary MacDonald became embroiled in a bitter, international child custody fight, an editor searched in vain through the "M's" for her picture; he knew we had it, because we had already run it once. He did not find it, though, because the librarian had put it away under "S,' according to its original caption, "Scotch Lass."

Everyone who remembers the old days has his favorite morgue story. Mine goes back to when I covered my first beat, the state employment office. One of my weekly chores was to write a brief item telling how many unemployment insurance claims had been filed in San Jose. After some months of this, I was asked to do a piece tracing the joblessness curve for the past half year or so, and the obvious way to get the information in a hurry was to consult my weekly stories for the period in question. But in the "Employment" file I could find only about half of them; the rest were missing.

Finally the librarian solved the mystery. He informed me, arguing that his system was the soul of logic, that in weeks when the claim level dropped, he filed my stories under "Employment;" when it rose, he filed them under "Unemployment."

Long-time readers of any paper, even if they detest it, develop a sense of proprietorship about it. They feel privileged to excoriate the editor, critique the columnists, and second-guess the reporters. Their wont finds its most visible expression in the letters column, but its loudest expression in their howls when they miss their papers.

The newspaper business is a paradoxical one wherein vast sums are expended for the best efforts of highly trained professionals and specialists—whose final product is entrusted to an adolescent (and perhaps a delinquent), the carrier. He or she can make or break the whole operation.

Christie Barrie, who has been fielding complaints in the *Mercury News* circulation department for years, knows that subscribers are a sensitive lot. Some are boors and dingbats, but most are good-hearted folk who crave tender loving care, such as the woman who called in with special instructions for her carrier: "Tell him to go down the driveway to the third window; it will always be open. Tell him to toss the paper in the window *gently*. Tell him not to throw it; it must *not* be thrown. My bed is just inside the window. If he tosses it gently it will land on my bed. I have my coffee and a sweet roll on the table next to my bed. That way

I can read the paper at breakfast without getting up."

Our circulation department will long remember the newcomer to Willow Glen who called in to subscribe, giving an address on "Crescent Drive—as in moon."

"How do you spell that?" Circulation asked, just to be sure.

"M-O-O-N," the caller replied.

Christie has found subscribers to be sensitive about where they live, witness the complainer who missed a paper at an address in Los Altos.

"Is that a private residence or an apartment?" Christie inquired.

"Didn't you hear me?" snapped the caller in a voice dripping like an icicle. "I said *Los Altos*. Only the elite live in Los Altos, and we all live in *homes*. Imagine you, a mere clerk, suggesting that I live in an apartment."

The flip side of that call was one from a woman who, starting the paper, gave an address in Los Altos Hills. Circulation couldn't locate the street, however, and called her back for better directions. Sheepishly she replied. "I live in Alviso. My husband told me to say Los Altos Hills. He said *never* to tell anyone we live in Alviso."

Some subscribers personalize their relationship with the newspaper. One woman announced, "My name is Mrs. Bell. All my friends call me Ding Dong." Another, asked her name, said, "Just call me Grandma. Everybody does."

As a class, newspaper people tend toward inflated egos; so it is probably salutary that readers deflate them occasionally. For a long time we thought the ultimate call of that genre came from a man who told us, "Yesterday I was roaring drunk and ordered the paper. Today I'm cold sober and I don't want it."

But that was topped by the reason a San Jose woman gave for stopping the paper:

"My bird has died; so I don't need it any longer."

CHAPTER VII
Typos And Bloopers

Error-prone words...sharp-eyed readers...missing letters...perils of juxtaposition.

In the mid-1970s the *Mercury News* was in the vanguard of the newspaper industry's stampede from hot type to computerized phototypesetting. Gone were the rattling Linotypes and the inky aroma of the composing room, replaced by the green glow of video tubes all over our shop. Our public relations people cranked out a series of "house ads" telling readers how this wondrous new technology would improve their newspapers. One copywriter, carried away, wrote that typographical errors would disappear.

They didn't, of course, and happily so, for as the *New Yorker* magazine long ago discovered, the typos often provide the best reading in the newspaper.

Probably the *Mercury's* all-time classic appeared on its society page about 20 years ago in a story about a girl's engagement party:

A summer wedding is in the offing for Jane Doe, whose enlargement was told at a dinner party in the home of her parents.

The police beat produced a notable specimen for my typo collection (every reporter has one) in 1973 under the headline "$37,000 Stolen From Hidden Safe." The story was unexceptional until the fifth paragraph, which read:

Police said the wife had not been broken into but appeared to have been opened with the combination.

In the experienced journalist's mind, a red flag goes up every time he uses any of several words he knows to be error-prone. Probably the most common is "public," which has a way of losing its "l," as in this exemplar from the *Mercury*:

The park district was formed by voters in November to acquire, preserve, and manage open space for pubic use from Los Gatos to Palo Alto.

Another dangerous word is "bridge," which with remarkable regularity loses its "g," as it did in the *Mercury* around 1950, in a wire story out of Yugoslavia about an attempt on the life of Marshal Tito. A band of partisans, the paper reported, had "mined a bride over which Tito was scheduled to pass."

The alacrity with which *Mercury News* readers find and report typos is proof that every word in the paper, no matter how obscure, is read by someone. It didn't take the customers long to tell us about these:

—From the Sunday auto page: "The dealer must fully inform you if there is a reasonable expectation that eternal repairs can correct your transmission problems."

—From an AP dispatch out of South Dakota: "Calvary Sgt. Albert Knaak rested in peace—but without honor—for 81 years." ("An old Roman soldier, no doubt," a reader observed.)

—From the caption of a five-generation birthday photo of a 91-year-old woman, with her daughter, granddaughter, great-granddaughter, and great-great-granddaughter: "Other will-wishers are, left to right,…etc."

—From a Western Appliance ad for microwave ovens: "500 watts of cooking power cooks almost everyone in one-third the usual time."

—From a "People" item about the late Sen. Hubert H. Humphrey, who was renowned for his windy speeches: "Humphrey, 65, had his blatter removed last Thursday."

—From a full-page "house ad" honoring the papers' own home delivery district managers: "These individuals were awarded a silver ring and a special plague."

—From an advertisement for a new Mexican restaurant: "To bring our infamous Mexican food a little closer to Eastern Santa Clara County, we have opened a beautiful new Casa Verde, complete with cocktail lounge and live entertainment."

—From a Long's Drug ad: "Cymbidium Orchids, packed in a foil box with water vile and ribbon."

—From *Mercury* wire reports of Pope Paul's illnesses in the mid-1970s: A series of references to his "prostrate disorder."

—From a classified ad for tools: "Vice, $10."

—From a press release issued by Assemblyman Alister McAlister, recruiting candidates for the California Maritime Academy: "The graduate…may, if qualified, receive a commission as an ensign in the U.S. Navel Reserve."

"Grisly" is a word fraught with peril for California journalists, who too often give it the ursine character of the state animal. Foolishly I once chided the *Spartan Daily* when, in a piece about the 1933 lynching of the Brooke Hart kidnappers in St. James Park, it related, "A spotlight trained on the tree highlighted the grizzly execution." The student staffers at San Jose State were quick to bombard my glass house with stones; a year earlier, the *Mercury* had committed the identical sin, not deep in an inside-page story as the *Daily* had, but in a front page headline. Moreover we had compounded our own felony. After a teenager had discovered a body near Lexington Dam, our headline had proclaimed, "A Grizzly Discovery by Youth." We had changed it in the next edition, of course—to "A Grizzly Murder in the Mountains."

Akin to the typographical error is the grotesque juxtaposition. Two innocuous pieces of copy end up side by side with devastating effect. It was with this peril in mind that the late managing editor Bill Albee of the *Mercury* warned me when I was a cub, "Always send out more than enough copy for the Saturday church page. If you don't the printers will always fill it up with a rape or an ax murder."

As a journalistic aberration, the juxtaposition is more cherished by collectors than the mere typo. The latter reflects some poor devil's mistake (or occasionally, sabotage); the former, almost invariably, is pure, unforeseeable coincidence.

A few years ago the *Mercury* carried a story from San Benito County, about messy birds, headed "Pigeon Population Pains Hollister." The headline writer had no way of knowing it would run above an AP story from Cincinnati headed "Former Congressman Hollister Dies."

Another notable example cropped up in the *Mercury* when a story about Sen. Alan Cranston, a track star in his college days, appeared immediately to the right of an ad for Mennen's foot powder. The result:

FOOT ODOR? Cranston Has Always Run Hard

Even more memorable was the effect when, years ago, the *Mercury* used a bright little story about hijinks in the State Legislature as a filler. It appeared just above an ad for a San Jose chiropractor. Alas, the final paragraph of the story as written got lost somewhere in the back shop, and in type the whole thing came out like this:

SACRAMENTO (AP)—State Sen. Thomas Keating, San Rafael, who is seeking a Marin County judgeship, today got his campaign off with a clatter.
Fellow Sen. James McBride, Ventura, paraded around the Senate chamber wearing a large tin plate reading:

PILES
Itching – Burning – Bleeding
Rectal Disorders
Office Method of Treating
No Shots – No Surgery
No Loss of Time from Work
Dr. John Doe, D.C., office 122
E. San Salvador St. CY3-0000

In the days of hot type, when newspaper pages were cast from assembled Linotype slugs, errant slugs often turned up in the wrong stories. This happened in a 1969 item in the *News*:

> San Jose attorney Bernard J.
> He was booked into City Jail
> Allard has been named a "diplo-
> mate" by the American Board of
> Trial Advocates.

The first edition front page of the *News* for February 18, 1979, is an item for juxtaposition aficionados. The banner headline was on a wire story from Washington about HEW proposals to rectify alleged sexual discrimination in Social Security benefits. The Number 2 story was off the police beat. When the paper came out, here is what it looked like:

MORE MONEY FOR WOMEN

Hookers Arriving
In S.J. in Droves

Without question the prize exhibit in my collection has to be a 1952 photo from the San Francisco *Examiner's* society page. It is not, strictly speaking, a juxtaposition item, but it is akin to that genre, and there was no way in the world anyone in the *Examiner* shop could have seen it coming. On the day in question, the paper happend to be laid out with the society page and the comics back to back. Also on that day there were obviously problems in the pressroom—too much ink and too much pressure on the rollers—for the comics showed through clearly on the reverse side of the paper. And that's how it came to pass that an X-ray-like image of a newborn babe, from a cartoon, is visible squarely in mid-belly of a bride clad in virginal white, on the arm of her father, awaiting the march to the altar in a church in San Mateo.

For the newsmaker, as opposed to the newswriter, the counterpart of the typographical error is the slip of the tongue. It is the insidious foe of the politician's official dignity, and it is most likely to betray him when he is aroused and angry.

San Jose Councilman Joe Colla was angry when he shouted during a meeting, "The taxpayers are revolting—and I'm personally revolting, too!"

Ex-Mayor George Christopher of San Francisco was angry when he proclaimed, during his luckless 1966 bid for the governorship, "When I become governor, the first thing I'll do is restore some moral turpitude in this state!"

On another occasion the agitated Christopher, a mean metaphor mixer, warned his fellow Republicans against retreat into hidebound conservatism: "We cannot afford to so decapitate ourselves that we become impotent."

Jose Zertuche, once chairman of the Santa Clara County Democratic Central Committee, was annoyed with its behavior when he declared, "We're closing the barn door after the milk is spilt."

Former HEW Secretary Robert Finch, moodily surveying the overcrowded field in his 1976 race for United States senator, lamented, "We have a veritable stable of candidates in the minuet." (A dark horse from the stable, Sam Hayakawa, beat him.)

Public speakers often fall prey to the involuntary spoonerism, a peculiarity of diction involving transposition of sounds or syllables. It takes its name from the Rev. William A. Spooner of Oxford, in whose sermons a "crushing blow" emerged as a "blushing crow," and "sons of toil" became "tons of soil."

In the Patty Hearst trial, prosecutor James Browning Jr., furious about the press agentry of Patty's lawyers, asked the judge for a gag order to curb their "out-of-state courtments." At a state Democratic convention a few years ago, a delegate wearied by an interminable parliamentary hassle cried out, "Enough of this pecky bittering!"

Francis Lindsay, once a state legislator from the Central Valley (seatmate of San Jose Assemblyman Bruce F. Allen, now a judge) was a sort of walking spoonerism. People had trouble remembering whether he was Assemblyman Lindsay from Loomis or Assemblyman Loomis from Lindsay.

When one talks faster than he thinks or vice versa, falling into the spoonerism trap is all too easy, I can aver from sad experience. Blushingly (like Spooner's crow), I recall a state Republican meeting during the 1964 primaries, with an up-and-coming northern congressman as guest speaker. He dropped into the pressroom and, straddling a folding chair backwards, held an impromptu, bantering news conference. Trying to phrase a question about the party's upcoming national convention, I asked disastrously, "Who do you think is ahead for the nomination—Goldfeller or Rockewater?" I'm afraid I badly disconcerted the congressman—whose name was Gerald Ford.

The spoonerism is not always involuntary, of course. It was purposeful on the part of the fan who once wrote to the late *Mercury News* sportswriter Bud Stallings, transposing his consonants.

When State Attorney General Evelle Younger ran against Jerry Brown, in 1978, he was harried by two issues. He had miffed many of his fellow Republicans by voting, as a member of the Judicial Appointments Commission, to seat Rose Bird as chief justice of the State Supreme Court. And he was caught in a crossfire between "save the redwoods" environmentalists and the lumber industry. So when he was challenged on the latter issue by a sawmill worker, he bumbled,

"Next to Rose Bird, the redwoods have cost me more sleep than anything."

In 1977 an ex-mobster who reportedly had a $500,000 contract on his life was understandably agitated when he told UPI, "I know what the Mafia can do to a man who has crossed it. One day you wake up and find your head in one room and your legs in another."

And a San Jose letter-to-the-editor writer was disgusted with politicians and bureaucrats across the board when he wrote, "It is time to burn the butts off the sacred cows and fatted calves by igniting the dead wood that is bleeding us to death."

The newsmaker who manages to avoid self-crucifixion by twisted phrasing remains vulnerable nonetheless to the bloopers of others. The late Ivy Baker Priest, who served as both treasurer of the United States and California state treasurer, was a facile (and tireless) speechmaker. But once when she encountered a faulty public address system, the nemesis of many orators, the toastmaster compounded her grief with a lame effort at apology: "I'm sorry, ladies and gentleman, but we seem to have a screw loose in our speaker."

Some politicians have a knack for turning their garbled syntax to their advantage. When ex-Assemblyman Charles Meyers of San Francisco was charged during a campaign with using his office supply allowance to pay babysitters, he brushed off the accusation with, "I'm confident the public will see through the facts." He went on to easy re-election.

About 25 years ago San Jose had a councilman who won his seat with a quarter-page newspaper ad promising to show "no impartiality to anyone." And he was too smart to let a good thing get away from him; he repeated the identical promise four years later and was re-elected.

Of course writers are fully as capable of bloopers as are those they write about. The evidence is copious:

—A *News* item from the North County bureau: "PALO ALTO—Four lame duck city council members have sung their swan song."

—A *Mercury* yarn about an "electronic dictionary," resembling a pocket calculator, developed by a firm in Cupertino. The lead asked rhetorically, "What would Daniel Webster think?" The desk man who edited the piece, who should have known that Noah Webster, not Daniel, wrote the dictionary, reinforced the error with his headline, "Litronix versus Daniel Webster."

—A quote from a 1980 weather story: "He said unexpected storms are expected this time of year."

—A biblical blooper on the business page: "It's a case of Goliath using public media for a slingshot."

—A 1977 headline in the *News*: "Jailed Pot Smokers Cut in Half by Law." ("Cruel and unusual punishment?" asked reader Nick Gonzales.)

—A report of a supermarket burglary wherein a clerk "was shot in the checkout stand." ("A most painful spot," commented Mary Jeanne Sauerwein.)

—A line from a story about campus cops in the San Jose State University summer school paper: "The officers are on duty 24 hours a day and are responsible for all crimes on campus."

Church bulletins are notorious for eyebrow-raising. Jim Sniadecki, the ex-49er and Peninsula restaurateur, reported this from a bulletin at St. Pius Church in Redwood City, when the sermon topic was listed ahead of the music:

WHAT MAKES GOD TIRED?
Sister Monica and the Choir

The California Trucking Association newsletter wandered into a syntactical minefield in denying that regulated carriers were inefficient because they commonly ran around empty. An ICC study, the newsletter said, showed that unregulated trucks were "twice as empty."

For years, a complaint of callers to Santa Clara County Animal Control was the difficulty in reaching a live human in an emergency. Usually a recording answered. It didn't help that the tape gave instructions for dealing with a "vicious dead animal."

For candidates on the campaign trail, especially presidential aspirants far from home, local customs, speech habits, names, and geography are ever-present perils. Sen. Eugene McCarthy's big issue in 1968, of course, was get-out-of-Vietnam. In a memorable gaffe at Stanford University, he derided fears "that Ho Chi Minh, if not stopped at the 17th parallel, will soon be on the beaches of Hawaii and in the lemon groves of Palo Alto."

Sen. Robert Kennedy recognized his vulnerability to similar hazards. Arthur Schlesinger Jr.'s biography of him tells how, as he stumped the Bay Area in his ill-fated campaign the same year, he avoided mentioning Marin County because he couldn't remember whether it was Ma-RIN or MAR-in. His caution forsook him, however, at a rally in San

San Jose Mercury News

A few weeks before his assassination in 1968, presidential aspirant Robert F. Kennedy prepares to board his plane at San Jose Municipal Airport. He partially hides short-haired Assemblyman John Vasconcellos, whose name Kennedy mangled. Attorney (now judge) David Leahy is at center; the author at right.

Jose's St. James Park when he introduced a leader of his local campaign, Assemblyman John Vasconcellos (Vascon-CEL-los). Before a huge throng, Kennedy paid glowing tribute to his "great friend, John Vas-CON-cellos."

The invariable press cliche for another Democrat of the same era, Gov. Pat Brown, was "amiable bumbler" (which changed, he noted with satisfaction

later, to "ebullient father" when his son Jerry became governor). Pat's most famous blooper came when an Eel River flood devastated much of the North Coast during his term. Preparing to ask the president for a disaster proclamation, he decided to overfly the stricken sector in a helicopter. On landing, he held a press conference during which he solemnly declared, "This is undoubtedly the worst disaster in California since I was elected governor."

Another Pat Brown *faux pas* is documented in an extant press release. In 1964 he announced an appointment to a county fair board, routinely circulating a release about it to all desks in the State Capitol press rooms. A few hours later a second handout appeared on every reporter's desk:

KILL! KILL! KILL!

The announcement of the appointment of Walton Roland Smith to the 1A District Agricultural Association Board of Directors is reported erroneously...The release says he was appointed to succed the late Fred Parr Cox. Mr. Cox is not deceased and has two years to serve on his current term on the board. Therefore, there is no vacancy and no appointment.

Probably the most effervescent specimen in my blooper collection originated not with an inept newsmaker but came innocently from the pen of a San Jose youngster who filled out a sex education questionnaire at school, as follows. The spelling is unaltered:

Q. What does the expression, "Clap is contagious," mean? Why would it be considered undesirable?

A. Well, it's like when your in church and people shouldn't aploud, or clap, like they do at bars and concerts and stuff, because if one clap starts, pretty soon most of the audienece does it and not everyone apprecates it. That is the part that would be undesireable. It robs the worship for sake of person.

CHAPTER VIII
Strange Bedfellows

When a reporter turns investigator, it helps if he knows whom he's investigating.

"Investigative reporting" is much honored in American journalism, especially since Watergate. Long before that episode, though, I fear I was responsible for setting the cause back for some years at the *Mercury News*. I went on a fishing expedition at the State Capitol and came up with some unexpected fish in my net.

It was in 1963, while covering the legislature, that I undertook a series, a 12-parter, titled "Money, Power, and Politics." The lead on the first article, which was headed "Strange Bedfellows in a Political Jungle," is as true today as it was then:

> California politics is power politics, and secret money supplies much of the power. It flows from hidden pools to elect the men who govern us and determine the kind of laws they enact.

What I tried to do in my narrative, based on months of research, was document a correlation between campaign contributions to legislators and their voting records. It wasn't exactly a new theme.

Inevitably, a major character in my story was Jess Unruh, then speaker of the Assembly with his eyes focused (as well they still may be) on the governor's office. Jess is state treasurer now, with an image of rugged, down-to-earth, common-sense management of his job. It is an image he has striven mightily to achieve. In 1963, as speaker, he came across as a bully ruthlessly climbing the political ladder over the bodies of countless victims.

Unruh was "Big Daddy" then. He weighed close to 300 pounds, about a hundred of which he has since shed with a regimen of diet cola. I was pretty much on target when I wrote, "Everything about the 40-year-old speaker—his build, his manner, his speech, and the office he holds—suggests massive power and the will to use it."

Jess was important in my series because he had found a new way of using lobbyists to solidify and expand his political base.

In the pre-Unruh era, a lobbyist had to court 80 members of the Assembly; now, with Unruh in iron-handed control of that body, the lobbyist needed to court only Jess. At campaign time Jess told him where to make his contributions—either directly to candidates and incumbents who were members of the Unruh team, or to a secret bank account controlled by the speaker, from which he could dispense the campaign largess personally. Either way, the recipients knew the money was coming to them by the grace of Jess Unruh, and they had best not step out of line lest they be cut off the next time around.

The contributors, for their part, won tacit assurance that their special concerns would be given full consideration in the legislative fray. Unruh could give such assurance because in the Sacramento scheme of things, any Assembly speaker wields enormous power. He appoints the committees, and he refers the bills to them. He may not always be able to guarantee the passage of a bill, but he can certainly kill one by sidetracking it into a committee that is unfriendly.

Though Unruh's control over special-interest campaign contributions was a matter of common talk in State Capitol corridors and beyond, it had never been documented in print or otherwise. No one could get a handle on it because the cash flowed from donors to recipients through devious channels.

My expose of these matters had its genesis when I was stopped in a corridor by a man whose name must still be shielded. Though he had a comfortable office of his own in the Capitol building, he didn't want to talk there. Even in that remote time, a decade before Watergate, he thought it might be bugged. So he took me for a stroll through the Capitol grounds. Out there, under the trees, he called my attention to a single line in a routine story the *Mercury News* had run earlier.

It was our custom, after each election, to run the names of all local candidates' major contributors, which in those days meant everybody who had given $50 or more. Even under the loose campaign reporting laws of that time, the list always ran three or four columns in eye-straining agate type, which only someone with an overweening interest in politics would wade through. We knew there were those who did wade through it, though, because the slightest error in this mass of microscopic print would be called to our attention by many readers.

My companion in the park that day was one of those who perused the whole list line by line.

"In your list of Al Alquist's contributors," he pointed out to me, "you ran the name of Oscar Archibald." (Name changed.)

Indeed I had, but it hadn't meant a thing to me at the time. I had scarcely noticed it. My informant went on to note that Archibald had given Assemblyman (now Senator) Alquist $800, his biggest contribution.

"Archibald," my friend said, "is Jess Unruh's bagman. He's the fellow who distributes the campaign money that Jess controls. Why don't you check out what he has given to other candidates around the state?"

Moving on this suggestion, I headed for the State Archives, then in the Capitol basement. I would spend days in that remote repository before I was through. Poring over the recent campaign statements of all 120 members of the legislature (40 senators and 80 assemblymen), I realized right away

Author's Collection
Jess Unruh campaigning for governor in Santa Cruz, 1970; the author at right.

I had struck a rich vein, a veritable Mother Lode, of political intrigue.

My informant's tip proved precisely accurate and pertinent. Archibald's name began popping up all over the place. Ostensibly a young, struggling lawyer in Los Angeles and a man of modest means, he had given not only the $800 to Alquist, but also substantial sums to other lawmakers all over the state: $600 in Richmond, $500 in Antioch, $1,000 in Fullerton, and unspecified amounts to senators and assemblymen or their opponents in places like Bakersfield, Tujunga, La Puente, Fresno, Ventura, San Diego, Los Angeles, Eureka, and Farmersville. Not only that, I soon discovered that Archibald had contributed in amounts ranging from $250 to $1,150 to at least 16 other candidates from San Francisco to San Diego, using the fictitious name "California Committee for Better Legislation."

I started making the rounds of legislators who had received these gifts, asking what they knew about Archibald. Some professed not to remember him at all, despite his generosity. But others acknowledged (reluctantly) he was Jess Unruh's agent. I learned too that before Archibald had graduated from law school five years earlier, he had been on Unruh's payroll for a time as an obscure legislative aide, and Jess had appointed him to the Democratic State Central Committee.

In investigative reporting, surprise is important. Once I started asking questions in the open, I had to move fast, rushing from one source to another before they could get together, compare notes, and agree on a cover story.

This applied not only to Unruh's beneficiaries, but also to participants in other "strange bedfellows" alliances I had found in the murky realm of campaign finance. For example, there was another front committee, "United for California," which distributed up to $5,000 each to conservative legislators, mostly but not all Republicans, who would vote to torpedo Gov. Pat Brown's tax program. This money came from a pool fed mainly by Southern California banking and business interests.

At this point I knew I had the makings of a good story. But ahead I could see weeks of work checking and cross-checking my raw information, interviewing all concerned, and tying down loose ends. I took what I had back to San Jose for a conference with my editors, who told me to drop everything else and work full-time on the expose.

One of the holes in my story was the origin of the money Archibald was delivering for Unruh. Without doubt it came from special interests, but which ones? Two or three days after I started nosing around in the open, the answer came to me in a way I could never have predicted.

At that time I shared space in the Capitol's press room suite with the Hearst papers and the Long Beach *Independent* and *Press-Telegram*, the latter being sister papers to the *Mercury News* in the Ridder group. The Long Beach publisher was Hank Ridder, half-brother to my publisher, Joe.

One morning the general manager of the Long Beach papers dropped by, ostensibly to visit his own Capitol correspondent, Jim McCauley, who sat at the next desk to me. He invited both of us up to the sixth-floor cafeteria for coffee.

After some opening pleasantries, I learned that the general manager was not there to see Jim at all; it was me he was after. He laid his facts on the table. I had unwittingly stirred up a hornet's nest in the Long Beach newspaper office because Archibald's "California Committee for Better Legislation" was a front for the Long Beach tidelands oil lobby, and Hank Ridder was its biggest contributor. In effect, I was investigating my own publisher's brother.

Long Beach had a lot at stake in the Legislature in the early 1960s. A vast pool of oil, often said to be $2 billion worth, lay beneath its harbor. About half a century earlier, before the presence of the oil was known, the state had conveyed these tidelands to the City of Long Beach for purposes of port development. Then, when the underwater bonanza was discovered, the state wanted it back. The oil royalties became the bone of contention in a running battle between the state and the city, and in every session of the Legislature, bills were introduced to reclaim the tidelands treasure for the state.

By contributing liberally to Unruh's slush fund, the Long Beach interests counted on derailing any such legislation. That in effect was what the general manager of the *Independent* and *Press-Telegram* told me over coffee. I think he assumed that this disclosure, coming from a top executive of the Ridder organization, would halt me in my tracks, dissuading me from further exploration of the embarrassing terrain I had stumbled onto.

I listened courteously, trying to hide my feeling of having been hit in the stomach with a brick. The coffee klatsch broke up on a note of cordiality, but the instant I parted from Jim McCauley and his boss, I raced for a telephone—not my own phone in the press room where Jim could overhear me, but a public phone in the Capitol's east lobby. I called San Jose and got Art Stokes on the *News* city desk.

"How's the investigation coming?" he asked.

"I've found where the body is buried," I told him.

"That's great."

"No, it's not."

"Why not?"

"The body is named Ridder."

Consternation reigned, and I was called back to San Jose for urgent consultations.

But if the Long Beach manager had imagined he could kill my story solely by virtue of his exalted rank in the Ridder hierarchy, he had not taken into account the fierce independence of the individual members of the Ridder clan. No Ridder ever told another Ridder how to run his newspaper, and my publisher, Joe, dug in his heels.

Up to that point, so far as I know, Joe knew little about his brother's oil politicking in Long Beach, nor did he fully appreciate the stakes involved. So, after hearing the whole story of my encounter with Hank Ridder's general manager, he renewed the go-ahead on my investigation.

In fact, I inferred, it was not without a perverse delight that he did so. Joe and Hank Ridder differed politically and had backed opposing candidates in the previous year's Pat Brown–Richard Nixon race for governor. Joe was still smarting over an expose the Long Beach papers had undertaken in that campaign, of what would become a celebrated issue, the Howard

Hughes loan to Nixon's brother. Joe was and would remain through thick and thin a loyal Nixon friend. So in my series he saw a chance to get even with his brother on that score.

"We'll show him we can play politics, too," Joe said.

My "Money, Power, and Politics" series began in our Sunday paper two or three weeks later. An unflattering picture of Unruh accompanied the first article.

In 1963 the *Mercury News* had not yet reached full stature as a leading metropolitan paper, and if Jess had played it cool, my revelations would have been at most a passing sensation, scarcely noticed outside San Jose. Though my stories depicted Unruh as the tough political manipulator he was, and something of a bully, they disclosed nothing illegal, or even unethical according to the rough-and-tumble rules by which politics was then played.

But thin-skinned Jess, striving to improve his image and looking toward a near-future race for governor ("the new Unruh"), felt threatened and panicked. Not only had he been the instigator of the Long Beach papers' effort to kill my series, but when it started to run anyway, he inadvertently gave me my best publicity. In the Assembly Chamber, he made several disparaging comments about me from the rostrum, and in a chance meeting between us in the lower bar of the El Mirador Hotel, across the street from the Capitol, he derided the *Mercury News* as a "two-bit paper." His rumbling voice was overheard by everyone in the bar, which was packed with legislators and lobbyists, and they all rushed out to buy the paper. The *Mercury News*, which normally sold eight to ten copies a day in Sacramento, for a time became the hottest item on the newsstands near the Capitol.

In spite of an angry confrontation or two, Jess and I kept our overall relationship civil if not exactly warm throughout the whole episode. We remained friends. This would turn out to be a circumstance of some consequence.

My series had been running four days and had already covered most of what I knew about Unruh, Archibald, and the "California Committee for Better Legislation" when I began getting disquieting feedback from my San Jose home office. Unruh and the Long Beach Ridders were pressuring the paper to kill my remaining eight stories (which ironically, though Unruh didn't know it, showed mainly that his enemies were doing the same things he was).

I learned on Wednesday that a "summit meeting" of everyone concerned with my series, except me, had been arranged for that evening in a San Francisco hotel. Joe Ridder would be there with a squad of his executives (my bosses), as would his Long Beach relatives and, of course, Speaker Unruh.

In my Sacramento hotel room that night, I could only wonder what decisions about me were being reached in the City by the Bay. My first word of what transpired there came the next morning, not from my home office but from Jess himself. I encountered him in midmorning in the third floor corridor of the Capitol. Great bags under his eyes told me that the showdown dinner had been a traumatic one, contentious and lasting into the early morning hours, with alcohol flowing freely.

"Well, Jess," I asked, "who won last night—you or I?"

"Hell, Harry," the speaker replied, "it was about a Mexican standoff."

Later that day, after talking to my editors, I concluded that Unruh's appraisal had been right on the mark. Both he and I had been wounded by the compromise that had been agreed upon, but neither of us mortally.

How the negotiations had proceeded, I have never learned precisely, but I gathered the Ridders had gotten from Unruh a strong message that unless he emerged from the episode with his aura of statesmanship intact, they could jolly well look elsewhere for protection of their $2-billion oil pool.

The best part of the package for me was that my series would continue, in the main as already written. The remaining stories however, would be downplayed. The bold banner headlines atop page one would cease, and the rest of the stories would start well below the fold, beneath modest heads. Further, I was to abandon any follow-up on the original series; this was a considerable concession, because my work to date had produced tips that might have uncovered a lot of other Sacramento skulduggery.

Most galling to me, of the San Francisco Summit's terms, was an agreement that I should rewrite and soften my twelfth and final article, specifically to exonerate Speaker Unruh of wrongdoing and repair any damage I had done to his image.

Even today, two decades later, that article reads strangely. It retracts not a word of what I had written earlier, but says none of it was "cause for shock." It absolves both Jess Unruh and the rightwing forces behind "United for California" of evil, and goes on to declare:

> There is nothing immoral about any private interest financing candidates who share its general philosophy, in the hope that some of that philosophy may be reflected in government. That is the way democracy works.

All of which is of course true. Still, it was not the

sort of clarion ending I had planned for my series. I went out with a whimper instead of a roar.

It took awhile for my pride to recover, but in truth Joe Ridder had given little in the face of enormous pressure at the San Francisco Summit. As long as he was publisher thereafter, however, he remained reluctant about other ventures into tough investigative reporting.

Weeks after my series was wrapped up, someone asked me if I hadn't prostituted myself with that last article.

"Well," I said, thinking about the $2-billion oil pool under Long Beach harbor, "if I had to be a whore, at least I got a good price."

CHAPTER IX
The Cop Shop And The Courts

In the police station and the trial courts, one confronts the meanness of the town and the bleakness in the lives of its losers. But sometimes there is laughter too.

Nothing in the lawbooks decrees that a courtroom must be a grim forum. Occasionally a spark is struck, as during a trial a few years ago before San Jose Municipal Court Judge Arvin Robb.

A bank teller was on the stand, testifying about a deranged woman who had approached his window stark naked.

"Did you notice anything unusual about her?" asked her attorney.

"Yes."

"And what was that?"

"She didn't have a passbook."

I would need a refresher course to go back to the police and court beat where I felt at home 30 years ago. Covering crimes and trials is much trickier now. "Fair trial" rulings by the higher courts, gag orders by the lower ones, and a sharpened sense of fair play on the part of the media themselves now circumscribe what is told.

We are not only fairer to suspects than we may have been once, but more protective of victims, because the times are meaner. We used to print routinely the addresses of crime victims, for instance, but now we seldom do because that sets them up to be hit again.

All in all, police and court coverage is probably better now than in the old days, but the improvement has carried a price; a lot of the flavor is gone.

The most colorful if least decorous of San Jose's judicial arenas a generation ago was the Police Court. It convened each morning in the old City Hall downtown, using the room which doubled at night as the council chamber. Presiding was the red-faced Irish Judge Percy O'Connor. Outside the courtroom his passion was florid patriotic oratory. He was a great welcomer for visiting conventioners.

Percy was, one might say, a pleasant bigot in the fashion of his day. Once, casting about for a line with which to greet a B'nai B'rith convention, he said, "You people know, I guess, the difference between a rich Jew and a poor Jew. A poor Jew washes his own Cadillac."

Reports filtered back to City Hall that the laughter at this line was very thin, prompting some wag there to observe, "That must have come from the poor Jews."

The clientele of Percy's court on any morning was a motley collection of still-boozy winos, prostitutes, and black-and-blue characters picked up for fisticuffs in bars during the night. Mixed in were undesirables who had committed no discernible improprieties but were *persona non grata* to the police and had been rounded up to be "vagged out of town." In the Great Depression, San Jose and other cities fought constantly to keep bums off their streets, using the

Percy O'Connor ran the Police Court.

vagrancy law under which anyone loitering without visible means of support could be hauled off to jail. The element of improper conduct, if any, was irrelevant. The usual penalty for vagrants, after their night in the hoosegow, was $10 suspended, provided they weren't caught again in the city limits.*

Percy O'Connor relished the showmanship opportunities of his judgeship. Once I was a spectator when a jury trial, a proceeding rare for that rough-and-tumble tribunal, was about to begin. Twelve citizens drawn by lot filled the jury box, and the judge and lawyers were conducting a cursory *voir dire* of their suitability.

Because veniremen filled all the seats in the room, I stood in the rear. Several prospective jurors were excused for various reasons, with others taking their place, until finally it appeared the panel was complete. Judge O'Connor's attention, however, focused on one juror, a young black man wearing white coveralls.

"Mr. Jones," the judge said, "I see you have work

---

*The efficacy of the vagrancy law, as enforced during the Depression, was dubious. It did not, in the long run, rid the streets of tramps; it only accelerated their rotation from city to city. Much later it came under attack by the American Civil Liberties Union and was declared unconstitutional by the United States Supreme Court in 1983.

clothes on. Will it be a hardship for you to take time off today?"

The man replied that in fact, it would.

"Then you're excused, Mr. Jones," O'Connor said. A replacement was quickly seated, and the trial got under way.

A few minutes later, while the lawyers were presenting their opening arguments, Percy beckoned me, in the midst of the proceedings, to approach the bench. Mystified, I did so. There was a wicked glint in the judge's eye as, oblivious to the attorneys' droning, he whispered to me with his hand over his mouth, "Pretty neat—the way I got that jig off the jury, wasn't it?"

Among the more colorful characters around San Jose courtrooms for many years was the late Frank Sauliere, flamboyant reporter *par excellence* for the *News*. Frank was an iconoclast, individualist, and militant fighter against injustice, but he had essentially conservative tastes, invariably wearing a dark suit and an old-fashioned black string necktie on his rounds.

Once during a grand jury investigation of civic corruption, Sauliere returned to the office with virtually verbatim notes on a three-hour session of the jury, held by law in secret in a locked courtroom. The late Jack Wright, managing editor of the *News*, wanted to know how he had obtained the material.

"Well," Frank said, "the jury was down in the audience seats, and I was down under the judge's bench where he puts his feet. If I'd sneezed, they'd have caught me."

Had he been caught, Frank was prepared to complain that he habitually snoozed under judges' benches and that the jury had greatly inconvenienced him by trapping him there.

Unfortunately, Wright deemed Sauliere's story too hot to handle under the circumstances by which he had obtained it, and it never saw print.

Sauliere regularly regaled the newsroom with behind-the-scenes yarns from the courts, notable among which was the tale of the thirsty attorney. The episode, as he told it, took place in the pre-air conditioning era when the courtrooms often became furnaces in summer. On this occasion a young lawyer earnestly pleading his case was suddenly overcome by a parched throat.

On the judge's bench was a tray with a decanter of ice water and several tumblers. Quite naturally the lawyer paused in mid-argument, excused himself to the court, and strode over to the bench and poured himself a glass from the decanter. He took a deep swig of it.

At this point, Sauliere said, there was an awkward pause in the proceedings. After what appeared to be a curious spasm, it took the young lawyer several minutes to get back on track with his argument. But the normally cantankerous judge, demonstrating unusual compassion, took no notice and shortly thereafter called a recess.

Little wonder—for at this point the judge and the lawyer shared a secret to which no one else in the courtroom was privy. The judge's decanter had contained not ice water, but the four-to-one martini mix from which His Honor habitually sipped during the afternoon. Counsel had inadvertently discovered the judge's nipping; and the judge, for his part, knew the young attorney was laboring under a mighty disability, having just gulped about six ounces of 90 proof gin and vermouth.

Awaiting a jury's return is always an ordeal for all concerned. One such wait followed the long, tense 1950 trial of a Saratoga man accused of slaying his wife under circumstances that, as they came to light in testimony, generated considerable sympathy for him. She had been no prize. Nevertheless, his alleged offense was of utmost gravity, and the murder and trial had been a top story in every Northern California paper for months. Suspense ran high on a Saturday morning as the jury neared a verdict.

The defendant was a newcomer to Saratoga from somewhere in the Southwest, where he had vast range and cattle holdings. Drawing on inherited wealth, he retained eminent counsel, George T. Davis of San Francisco. As a young man Davis had made his name as a criminal lawyer in the "American Dreyfus case." He had freed Tom Mooney, the international labor *cause celebre* imprisoned 22 years on trumped-up evidence as the bomber of San Francisco's World War I Preparedness Day parade.

Reporters were bantering with Davis as they sweated out the verdict on the cattle king. One of them asked Davis whether, if his client were convicted, he would represent him in an appeal or a new trial.

At that point the lawyer wasn't sure, but he said, "If I do, I want one favor from you fellows. All through this trial, in every story, you have referred to 'the wealthy cattleman and his attorney, George T. Davis.' If I represent him in a second trial, I want you to change that for the sake of accuracy. Next time make it 'the cattleman and his *wealthy attorney*, George T. Davis.'"

The district attorney in the cattleman's case, Napoleon J. Menard, was one of the most combative lawyers ever to star in a San Jose courtroom. Nap was the epitome of the prosecutor—sardonic, truculent, tenacious. He could easily have served as the proto-

type for Erle Stanley Gardner's D.A. in the Perry Mason stories, Hamilton Burger.

Finally the time came, though, when Menard tired of strife in an adversary role and longed for robes of a judge. The governor at the time, who had a vacancy to fill on the Santa Clara County Superior Court, was Goodwin J. Knight, a Republican. Nap Menard was, alas, a Democrat, but that would not prove an insurmountable handicap. The proper contacts were made at Sacramento; Menard then paid a quiet visit to the registrar of voters' office and re-registered as a Republican. A few weeks later his judgeship came through.

I was covering the governor's office at the time and made it a point to get advance tipoffs on judicial appointments. In Menard's case I got the word a few

San Jose Mercury News

Napoleon J. Menard, prosecutor personified.

days early and paid Nap a visit for some background to flesh out the story when it broke. Under the ground rules we set up, unfortunately, our interview was off the record, and only substantive facts could be used when the appointment was announced.

We finally worked around to the question of Menard's successor as district attorney, to be appointed by the county supervisors. Ultimately, the political dynamics of the situation would cause Menard to bestow his public endorsement on Louis Bergna, who would hold the job for the next quarter-century. When I talked to him, however, he was rooting for his assistant and chief investigator, Angelo Pestarino.

"I'm proud of the way we've run this office," he said. "We never issue a complaint unless we know for a fact that someone is guilty in the first place. And Angie will follow that same policy."

In my mind a red flag went up. "But, Nap," I asked, "if you believe that, won't that put you in a bind when you're on the bench? Let's say you're hearing the criminal calendar, and Angie brings in a guy for murder or robbery or whatever. You as judge are certain he's guilty, as you've just said, or Angie wouldn't have him there to begin with. Haven't you prejudged the case? What does this do to the presumption of innocence?"

Menard's lip curled as he replied, in a line that would produce mass apoplexy in today's ACLU, "Well, you know, Harry, the presumption of innocence is just a legal fiction anyway."

This prosecutorial mind-set did not seem to impair Menard's later performance on the bench. His tenure there was short, though, brought to an untimely end by his death after surgery in 1960.

One of the more reprehensible practices of some newspapers is to dredge up periodically the crime sensations of time past for the titillation of new readers. It is cruel practice, for there are always people around who were close to these stories and can be hurt by their retelling.

That was the reason I waited almost two decades before I retold, in a 1978 column, what I called "The Case of the Framed Rapist." By then (I thought) everyone who had had anything to do with the case was dead. The man who had been wrongfully sent to prison had been dead 18 years, but I still chose to call him "Joe Doakes." Also long gone were the judge, William F. James; the district attorney, Menard; the defense attorney (later judge), Ray Callaghan; the sheriff, Howard Hornbuckle; and the News' police reporter, Ralph Condon.

The case had all the ingredients of a much later crime story, Watergate: obstruction of justice, cover-up, nocturnal spying, an activist role of the press. And in the end (I wrote) "justice triumphed."

The story began in 1947 with a rapist loose in San Jose. He would accost young women at bus stops, force them into his car at knifepoint, rape them on lonely roads, and then release them. He struck four times within a year.

Finally, in June, 1948, police arrested Doakes, a meek Santa Clara cement worker. The main evidence against him was the absence of a right rear fender on his car, a deficiency one of the victims had mentioned. Within four months Doakes was indicted, tried, convicted, and sentenced to 75 years in San Quentin.

From the start, certain things about the prosecution of Doakes didn't ring true. Yet he would serve a year and seven months before being freed in 1950 at the end of a retrial ordered by the Court of Appeal.

"Fair trial" has come a long way since 1950. Now there are "discovery" rules requiring the prosecution to share its critical evidence with the defense. Then each side guarded its secrets jealously, hoping to confound the other with a "surprise witness" or a "bombshell." So, during Doakes' first trial, defense attorney Callaghan had been denied access to the statements the rape victims had originally given to the sheriff. In a roundabout ways, word had gotten out that the prosecution had a reason for hiding these statements: they would demolish the state's case. With the retrial approaching, Callaghan's obvious problem was to get his hands on them, and for help, he turned to the late Ralph Condon, police reporter for the News.

Condon, who had a strong sense of justice and also enjoyed a caper, had free run of the sheriff's office. He could rummage through the files at will. One night while the appeal was pending, he "borrowed" the Doakes file for a few hours. It was taken to Callaghan's office or some other rendezvous, thence to a cooperative photostat shop where the night was spent copying the documents page by page. (The Xerox era of instant photocopies was years in the future.) By the morning, Condon had replaced the file in its accustomed repository.

As hoped and expected, the copied documents dealt a death blow to the prosecution. One victim, in her original statement to the police, had told of trying to resist. She had reached down between the seats of the car, she said, hoping to find a tire iron or other weapon. The prosecution hadn't let *that* come out during the first trial—because Doakes' car had a bench seat with no space in the middle. Other new evidence established that on the date of one rape, Doakes' automobile had been in a Lincoln Avenue garage for repairs after a wreck.

On the final day of the second trial, Condon was in the courtroom as an understandably interested spectator; I was with him. We were standing against the wall of the hushed chamber, perhaps 20 feet from the door, as District Attorney Menard wound up his final argument. With his evidence in disarray, he was falling back on dramatics.

"You women of the jury," he intoned, fixing each woman in turn with his eye, "can you imagine your feelings if assaulted by this *monster*?" He pointed to the smallish Doakes, cowering at the defense table like a frightened rabbit.

As Menard neared his climax, with the jury's attention riveted on him, Condon whispered, "I think this is a good time for me to leave."

Ralph was a towering, solidly built outdoorsman who weighed about 230 pounds. As he turned and plodded toward the courtroom door with the deliberate gait of Frankenstein's monster (clomp!, clomp!, clomp!), every eye in the jury box turned his way. Whatever eloquent peroration Menard might have prepared was lost forever.

Three hours and 15 minutes later, the jury found Doakes innocent on all counts.

As I mentioned, when I told the foregoing story in column form in 1978, I thought everyone connected with it was dead. But a few days after it ran, I got a letter from Steven A. Walker of Los Gatos, then 35, a social worker with the Santa Clara County Department of Mental Health. Joe Doakes, whose real name was Frank "Bunny" Walker, had been his uncle, and Steven remembered being taken to San Quentin, as a small child, to visit him.

Steven Walker was not entirely happy with my narration of his uncle's story, though not for the reasons I might have expected. He wrote:

Although I found it consoling to have this story publicly aired, I am troubled by much of what you implied.

First of all, I do not accept that this story can now be told (only) because all the participants are dead. We should remember that it was largely because he was protected from rigorous public scrutiny of his abuse of power that the district attorney who framed my uncle soon became an "honorable" judge.

Second, I do not accept that "in the end, justiced triumphed." My uncle was terrorized by a vigorous investigation and prosecution for a crime he never committed...He then went to San Quentin for the practical application of his sentence.

Rape of an adult woman is a high-status crime in prisons today, a crime for which most of those convicted receive light sentences. When my uncle went to prison, rapists were routinely beaten and gang-raped. Frank Walker left from his 19 months in prison a terribly traumatized man who would never fully recover from his punishment.

Tonight I will watch "Holocaust" for much the same reason I write this letter. The Nuremberg trials did not provide anything approaching a triumph of justice for European Jews...

I write to encourage people not to forget that nothing can make up for the unthinkable suffering endured by the innocents of ruthlessly self-seeking public officials and institutions.

Finally, who is being protected by not revealing "Joe Doakes's" name? Bunny remains my most cherished uncle. I and the rest of my family feel the greatest love, compassion, and respect for Bunny.

Do not do us the injustice of this "protection."

San Jose Mercury News

The First National Bank, at the southwest corner of First and Santa Clara Streets, was San Jose's first skyscraper. It still stands, with a new look and a new name (see page 69). In this early-1920s view, at least one horse-drawn rig (black arrow) competes with autos for parking space on South First Street between Santa Clara and Post.

CHAPTER X
Columns, Cornices, And Concrete

Tears were shed when they razed San Jose's bastard-baroque City Hall of 1887. But will anyone mourne a century hence when they tear down the county's "rust bucket" tower?

Tracing San Jose's skyline, one turns back time decade by decade.

Of course "skyline" is a word that until lately was a bit pretentious for San Jose, whose expansion has been more horizontal than vertical. Our buildings have tended to hug the valley floor, much as the adobes of the 18th century did. But our skyward growth has burgeoned in the past 10 years.

Our towers of the 1980s run to steel and mirror glass, which produces wavy murals of ever-changing, spectacular cityscapes and cloudscapes.

Such effects were presaged in the 1970s in the 13-story County Administration Building, with mirror facades on east and north, but deliberately rusted steel for its other two sides. The county supervisors were flimflammed into accepting the steel in the supposed interest of cheap maintenance. The sad consequence is that from the south and west the building resembles a destroyer from the mothball fleet sitting on its fantail.

The 1950s and '60s were the era of raw concrete, poured or assembled in pre-stressed panels by architects whose imaginations were limited to the cube and the oblong block. Many of them worked in the state architect's office in Sacramento; hence the sterile packing-crate style of the perimeter buildings at San Jose State University. They were designed with sturdiness and square-feet-per-dollar as the

prime considerations, but one of them, a library facing Fourth Street, flunked even those tests. No sooner was it occupied than the concrete began to sag under the weight of the books, and the state was put to fabulous cost jacking and shoring it up. For some years thereafter it was known as Swayback Hall.

Architecturally, there is not much in San Jose to represent the war-torn 1940s. Toward the end of the decade, however, the monolithic Penney's Building went up at the northwest corner of First and Santa Clara Streets, where the 19th-century Knox Block had stood. Its designers seemed to have taken their inspiration from the Maginot Line pillboxes, breaking the monotony only with a row of tiny, embrasure-like windows just below roof level. Esthetically, the kindest thing ever said about the building (prior to a major restoration and face-lift under way at this writing) was that it had "clean lines." A *News* editorial called it "Fort Penney."

A revival of the tile-roofed, early-California motif marked the depression-ridden 1930s, when San Jose civic architecture got a push from Franklin D. Roosevelt's Public Works Administration. Important PWA projects included the Civic Auditorium, built for $600,000 including the site. What was originally the main Post Office (now the St. James Park substation) dates from the same era and seems to be an ornate transmutation of the padres' humble style into alien materials, with not even a suggestion of white-washed adobe. Instead the Post Office is faced in glazed, beige terra-cotta tile. That materials and labor were cheap in the '30s is evidenced by the fact that this facing is on all four sides of the building, even out back next to the loading docks, and the whole edifice cost $256,000. They don't build 'em that way any more.

The 1920s and earlier decades were the true time of terra-cotta and brick, exemplified in the "old" Bank of America (originally Bank of Italy) Building, diagonally across from Fort Penney at First and Santa Clara. It was erected during a renaissance of classicism, complete with facade of Corinthian columns. Old-timers will recall, however, that the colonnade was bastardized for its first 20 years or so. Originally the bank needed only half the frontage, so it leased the rest to Roos Bros. But the clothing store needed display windows, not a Temple-of-Zeus entrance. So in the south half of the colonnade only the upper drums and capitals were installed, resting on a huge I-beam. The pedestals and lower drums were not added until Roos moved out. Today only a sharp eye can detect that these are probably the only Corinthian columns in the world built not from the bottom up, but from the top down.

Corinthian columns also grace the original County Courthouse on North First Street, a structure rich in history. Its cornerstone was laid in 1866, and it was overbuilt for the size of our pueblo at that time. It was crowned by a magnificent dome. This was not mere civic exhibitionism; San Jose still had hopes of regaining the State Capitol it had lost in 1851, and it might help to have a suitable building ready. Alas, that dream came to naught.

In 1931 a mid-afternoon fire (to which I, at age six, was an eyewitness) gutted the Courthouse. It might have been torn down then, had not someone with an appreciation for its classic lines decided they should be saved. The building was restored with its splendor essentially intact. In the restoration the portico was

When San Joseans laid the cornerstone for their Courthouse in 1866, they dreamed of its becoming the State Capitol. To its rear at left, the County Jail.

At the instant the dome toppled in the 1931 fire, a Mercury Herald *cameraman snapped his shutter. At right, the Hall of Records.*

San Jose Mercury News

The restoration, a happy mating of classic lines with California mission tile. The jail is still out back, left. In foreground, excavations for the Post Office where the old St. James Hotel had stood.

Hall of Records: First Street facade.

San Jose Mercury News

The new look: after 117 years the Courthouse, with white accents on chocolate brown, still serves. Check the growth of the palms since the time of the engraving, page 60.

lopped off and the columns were recessed into the facade. The dome was replaced by a needed third story topped by a tile roof, presumably to evoke a little of the town's Spanish heritage. Such blatant style-mixing could have produced a grotesque edifice, but the result was surprisingly harmonious and stately.

Earlier, the original Courthouse had acquired two annexes—a north wing called the Hall of Records and a squarish, homely blob of a building to the rear, the

Hall of Justice. Few if any tears were shed when the wreckers moved in on these buildings in the early 1960s. Neither was architecturally worthy of its juxtaposition to the 1866 structure.

Screams came later, however, when a new building, with additional Superior Court rooms, went up where the old Hall of Justice had stood at Market and St. James. Its architects faithfully retained all the ugliness of its predecessor, erecting a stark, truncated tower of concrete, unadorned saved for vast, window-less, vertical expanses of buff brick facing. This brick treatment worries retired engineer Ed Steffani, who for years was the county highway boss.

"The reinforced concrete building underneath is probably 'hell for strong,'" he says, "but what happens to the brick skin, fastened on with baling wire, in a good shake? If you're inside being tried, you're OK. But consider the poor guy who has just proved his innocence, only to walk outside and get buried under a pile of bricks."

Today the Superior Court, having grown tenfold since World War II, occupies three buildings in San Jose and outposts in other parts of the county. But the 1866 structure as restored still carries its share of the load. There is little dispute that it imparts more dignity to the judicial process than any building of later date.

The old City Hall downtown was prominently situated in the Plaza, where the Paseo de San Antonio intersects it today. When the time came in 1958 to tear the building down, there was a monumental battle in which the whole town chose up sides.

Leading the "save City Hall" forces was the late Lenore Fowler, in whose eyes the old brick edifice was beautiful. She was a pioneer aviatrix and the wife of Robert G. "Bob" Fowler, who had made the first west-to-east flight across the United States in 1911. (A plaque honoring him adorns the Municipal Airport terminal, and Robert Fowler Way at Reid-Hillview Airport is named for him.)

For years Lenore's shrill voice had enlivened many a squabble in the old council chamber, for she was a civic activist with strong ideas on most every issue. (Her tradition is carried on today by her letter-writing son-in-law, "Abil Layman," of whom I tell in the "Characters" chapter.) When Lenore tried to keep

San Jose Mercury News

Courthouse at Market and St. James: Just as homely as its predecessor.

When the old City Hall was new, the traffic outside was horse-drawn. Built in 1887 for $139,482, the building dominated City Plaza, separating West San Antonio Street (today's Paseo) from Park Avenue.

City Hall in the 1920s, from southwest. Vehicles outside are the police cars of the time. Frame of Bank of Italy Building (now Bank of America) in left distance, above palm tree.

"To a game fighter." For Lenore Fowler, Mayor Louis Solari inscribes the first brick removed from the old City Hall.

the wreckers from the old City Hall, she threw heart and soul into the fight. She acidly lectured the city councilmen by the hour, accusing them of "railroading" the demolition and hinting darkly at ignoble motives. "Those bricks must be pretty hot," she said. "Someone must want them pretty badly."

Mrs. Fowler was destined to lose her battle. She and William Ward, an old-time Agnew rancher, circulated a "save City Hall" petition but fell far short of the required signatures. There are still those in San Jose, including some too young to have ever seen the old building, who think Lenore was right. In 1980 a San Jose State student, Scott Hinrichs, looked backward to the 1950s through rose-colored glasses with less than 20-20 vision and wrote in the *Spartan Daily*:

> About five blocks west of SJSU a beautiful public building experienced its final death throes. Unfortunately the majestic old building with its Victorian-styled brickwork and stone gingerbread fell to the ground in the name of urban renewal, which was highly touted by the city fathers, the influential few, and a certain local newspaper.

Hinrichs started quite a hassle with his piece, which I quoted in my column. Patricia Fairchild wrote in, "I do not see the current City Hall as an improvement in any way." Phil Trounstine, the young man then covering the new City Hall for the *Mercury*, stopped by my desk and asked regarding the old one, "Dammit, Harry, couldn't it have been saved?"

The answer was that most San Joseans in 1958 felt about the old City Hall as I did, after covering it for six years: It was a dump.

There was nothing "majestic" about it. Though some pictures of it convey a bogus charm in retrospect, it was (unlike the old Courthouse) an architectural monstrosity. It marred the beauty of City Plaza, now the loveliest of downtown parks. Leveling it could only help matters. My feeling about it was shared by everyone I knew who worked in the place.

It had been built for $139,482 in 1887, a block of bastard-baroque masonry adorned with multiple cornices and surmounted by an overpowering Victorian cupola of no utilitarian value whatever. Its designers were the Lenzen brothers, Theodore and Jacob, whose name is still borne by a street off The Alameda. They seemed to specialize in monstrosities, judging by other of their buildings which survived till the mid-20th century. The American Institute of Architects rendered a sorry verdict on the old City Hall during the dispute over its demolition: "A design importation, reflecting a very bad period of German architecture. It is not typical of any period of design, and it is not a reflection of the art and culture of the community."

The ground floor, bisected by a weird east-west tunnel big enough to drive a car through, was the City Jail, with barred windows. The cell blocks were on the south side, and the drunk tank—malodorous from seven decades of boozy sweat, vomit, urine, and Lysol—was on the north. The city council chamber was one floor up, and the meetings were often enlivened by the banging of cell doors and rattling of bars below.

There was an elevator shaft but no elevator; the shaft was out of plumb, some said ever since the 1906 earthquake, though the lift was supposed to have creaked on for some years thereafter. Because there was no elevator, 1950-era Mayor Fred Watson, who had had a heart attack, risked another every time he climbed the steep staircase to the council chamber.

The old building's soft-mortar brickwork had cracks you could stick your finger into. They too had appeared in the 1906 temblor. A Rube Goldberg arrangement of reinforcing bars had been installed, but later engineering studies showed them to be useless. In the building's last years, everyone who worked there prayed the next quake would come at night so that the place could collapse without killing anyone (except, of course, the poor devils downstairs in the jail).

When the wreckers finally went to work on the building, after municipal offices had been relocated in the current City Hall at First and Mission, Lenore Fowler was on hand to obtain as a souvenir the first brick removed. Mayor Louis Solari inscribed it "To a game fighter."

In contrast to the $139,482 cost of the old City Hall, its replacement in the Civic Center bore a $2,546,774 price tag, with an annex costing another $3,800,000, not counting $400,000 for alterations. Sarah Winchester got off cheaper.

The history of the Civic Center, at First and Hedding Streets, is a classic study of how to take a prime architectural opportunity and botch it.

In 1948 most of the real estate we now call the Civic Center was a broccoli and cauliflower patch, little more than a mile from the center of town. That year, when the city and county bought it, the tab was only $198,000 ($3,000 an acre), but it was priceless in esthetic potential. Starting from scratch, the city and county could build on the pristine site an architecturally harmonious complex—the most efficient, beautiful, and impressive governmental center between Sacramento and Los Angeles.

Or so the argument went. People should have known better.

San Jose Mercury News

Civic Center, looking west, about 1957, with North First Street in foreground. City Hall's arc is taking shape. To its right, the first county office building at First and Hedding, torn down after barely 20 years to make room for today's "rust bucket" high-rise. At center, the first jail unit across Hedding Street from the two armories. Outlined in white, the Knoche grant, whose donor decreed it should remain open space forever.

Some of them, in fact, did, for they put up a ding-dong fight against the whole idea. They wanted to keep the seat of government downtown, either around the Plaza where City Hall was or around St. James Park where the Courthouse was.

Ignoring such opposition, the council and supervisors went ahead with the North First Street purchase anyway, without consulting the voters. When the site was belatedly put to a ballot test later in the year, it was roundly drubbed. But its proponents were not to be dissuaded; they got a ruling from the city attorney that the adverse vote was only "advisory," with no legal force. Two more elections were needed, in 1950 and 1952, before the voters' verdict was reversed and development could proceed.

Early in the game, a joint city-county steering committee was set up to oversee the Civic Center development and compel adherence to a master plan. At one point such a plan was actually committed to paper, including architects' renderings of stately, compatible city, county, and state buildings surrounding a park-like square. Somewhere that plan may still gather dust, in mute testimony to the glory that might have been.

The steering committee, however, never really got its act together, the main reason being that the city and county distrusted each other too much. One bone of contention was the exchange of property. Originally the county had purchased the northerly 44 acres of the site; the city the southerly 22. At that juncture no one had the foggiest notion of how the buildings would be laid out; so there was a "gentlemen's agreement" that land could be swapped back and forth between the two governments on an acre-for-acre basis as needed. Almost from the outset, though, the bureaucracy began to undercut the agreement, which broke down amid claims that "our acre is worth more than your acre." Each agency went its own way, and master planning went down the tubes—beginning with the "armory fiasco."

Long before either the city or county broke ground on the site, 14 choice acres were given away for the twin armories of the National Guard and Army Reserve. The unfathomable rationale was that since they would be public structures, the Civic Center was where they belonged. No one raised the point that an armory, at best, looks like a big barn. So the two buildings remain today on the north side of Hedding Street with their ceremonial artillery out front and their jeeps out back—utilitarian, noble in purpose, and ugly. As long as they stay, any plan for converting Hedding Street into a grand civic mall is illusory.

Apart from the armories, the Civic Center's first structure was a one-story county office building erected between 1951 and 1953 for $513,000. It was a fairly handsome edifice, with brick retaining walls around terraced gardens. But it was small, housing only a few departments, and never intended as the seat of county operations. It should have been tucked away in a remote corner somewhere. Instead, the supervisors in their wisdom located it at the main entrance to the center, at the southwest corner of First and Hedding. The upshot was that barely 20 years later this wholly worthy building, by then valued at several million dollars, was razed to make room for the $26 million tower of the County Administration Building, the most conspicuous landmark of the whole complex today.

No recitation of the Civic Center's misadventures would be adequate without a nod to the memory of Dr. Herman Knoche, who has been dead since 1945. A one-time Stanford professor and world-famous botanist, he owned a 16-acre field abutting the acreage that the city and county would acquire later. It was a long, slim parcel on an east-west axis, running from North First Street all the way to Guadalupe River.

Knoche was ahead of his time, an environmentalist who cherished open space in an era when "bigger and better" was the only byword for civic progress. So he bequeathed his field to the city with a single proviso: It must remain forever green, an open area where children could play. Otherwise it would revert to Knoche's heir, Gladys Switzer.

In accepting the bequest, City Manager John Lynch promised that San Jose would happily comply with the restriction. But nine years and two city managers later, City Hall was looking mightily for a way to squirm out of Lynch's commitment. By then the Civic Center was well on its way, and the city wanted to lump the Knoche land into the overall development. A deal was struck with Mrs. Switzer, who relinquished her reversionary right for $30,000.

So today Dr. Knoche's "children's park" is paved with asphalt; the Mission Street right-of-way on which the City Hall faces was carved from it.

Over the years the buildings of the Civic Center have risen helter-skelter, no two of them architecturally related. The seven-floor county building at Hedding and San Pedro is a stark monolith that someone has aptly likened to a Bekins warehouse. The City Hall was saved from barren rectangularity only by being "bent" into an arc. The jail resembles nothing more than a cluster of oversize cardboard cartons. The police building looks like a fort. And the Municipal Court completes the Oz-like scene with a facing of yellow bricks.

No one was more conscious of the hodgepodge than Tevis Dooley, the county's managing architect, when I talked to him about it. He had a convincing, and partially redeeming, explanation for it.

Most of the grand plans for the world's great cities,

he pointed out, were brought to fruition under dictatorships. Paris owes its splendor to Napoleon. The majestic design for Berlin by Albert Speer would have been a monument to Hitler. Washington was laid out, according to the plan of Pierre Charles

San Jose Mercury News

Today's sleek facades of the Bank of the West replaced buff brick and stone. For the building's old look, see page 58. The three-story wing at right was the pre-1942 home of the Mercury Herald *(compare with page 37).*

San Jose Mercury News

Looking north at pre-renewal South First Street, from between San Carlos and San Antonio. The year is 1960, and the tiny figure (arrow) in the open car crossing the San Antonio intersection is John Fitzgerald Kennedy. The architecture is a melange, and the southbound traffic direction is the opposite of today's.

L'Enfant, when Washingtonians lacked the vote and decisions could be imposed from on high. The San Jose Civic Center, though, has been subject to the vagaries of the democratic process every step of the way.

What many San Joseans, I among them, deem a heinous crime in the name of "progress" was the bureaucratic destruction of the old San Jose State Quad in 1963.

For half a century its ivy-clad, arcaded cloisters of gray stucco roofed with tile, surrounding a palm-studded lawn, had been the centerpiece of the campus. True, it was not a pure expression of any architectural style. Nonetheless, its designers had achieved a unique harmony, a setting of uncommon serenity and grace. It was also functional in that three sides of it were classroom wings.

As has been noted, however, Sacramento's architectural mentality dictated the eradication of every trace of individuality from state campuses, in favor of concrete masses reminiscent of Hitler's West Wall bunkers. The Quad, therefore, had to go. Someone in the capital decided any structure that old must be, *per se*, an earthquake trap.

The anguished alumni set up an outcry and won one victory; the Quad's focal point, the Tower ("La Torre"), was saved. But having lost that battle, the bureaucrats won the war. The wreckers descended on the rest of the quadrangle with a vengeance.

What followed was ironic justice. The demolition contractor lost his shirt because the old arcades were built like rock. Beneath the stucco was solid, diagonal board sheathing that made the structure essentially a monolith. It resisted the jackhammers, sledgeham-

mers, and bulldozers all the way. The consensus was that no earthquake, of any Richter rating, could have fazed it.

In fairness, the state has done an admirable job of relandscaping the acres where the Quad once stood, with a fountain, trees, and other adornments. But the old esthetics will never be approached, much less surpassed.

And what about the once-doomed Tower, rechristened "Tower Hall?" SJSU President Gail Fullerton worries not about its soundness. She has her office there.

San Jose State's Quad, as conceived by its architect in the first decade of the century. More than 50 years later, the demolition contractor lost his shirt.

CHAPTER XI
The Slaugterhouse War

If the pear orchards had to go, better that they were replaced by computer companies than by stock pens.

Whenever I ride north toward Alviso and the Bay, amid the sleek electronics plants that have replaced the former pear belt, I feel a touch of pride—even proprietorship. I miss the pear orchards as much as anyone, but the area's transformation over the past 15 years could have been much uglier. The greenbelt could have become not a handsome arm of Silicon Valley but, as Carl Sandburg called Chicago, "hog butcher to the world."

That prospect was real when, in 1966, I found myself deeply embroiled in San Jose's great Slaughterhouse War. The enemy (for which I held no malice then or now) was that billion-dollar giant of meat packing, Swift & Co. If *Mercury News* publisher Joe Ridder was the commanding general of the anti-Swift campaign, I was his guerrilla in the field. I was also writing the daily stories from the front line trenches.

For me the episode had an unlikely beginning. One late summer day I had gone to Los Angeles to cover some long-forgotten event, and at day's end I was in the newsroom of the Los Angeles *Times* writing my yarn; newspapers always extend hospitality to out-of-town reporters. No one in my home office knew where I was; so I was caught unawares when a light blinked on a phone at my elbow, and a *Times* staffer informed me, "It's for you." Our *Mercury News* PBX operator, with an unerring sixth sense, had tracked me down. It had to be some dire emergency. And so it

was, in the mind of Ken Conn, my editor, who was on the line. What he said in the next minute-and-a-half would launch me on a wacky adventure lasting for weeks.

"You live out on the north side of town, don't you?" he asked. He already knew I did, of course; I had lived for many years in Rosemary Gardens off North First Street. When I confirmed this, Ken said ominously, "Then you know you're going to be right downwind from this new Swift plant."

His allusion was to a story we had carried a few days earlier, to which I had paid only passing notice. But the piece, I now learned, had caused great anguish in our paper's front office.

The *Mercury News* was still downtown then, in the old shop at West Santa Clara and Almaden. Our present plant on Ridder Park Drive, off Nimitz Freeway, was under construction. The story that had panicked my bosses was an announcement from Swift, with great fanfare, of plans for a new "meat packing plant" that would be right across the freeway from us. It would employ 250 persons and "process" 5,000 head of cattle each week. The skids had been greased at City Hall, where an unofficial OK had already been given for the essential rezonings and use permits. Swift assumed the formal hearings on these matters would be cut-and-dried; it had been promised as much.

"No way!" said Joe Ridder. Undeceived by the

euphemistic rhetoric of Swift's announcement, he correctly perceived that his prospective cross-freeway neighbor (the "meat packing plant") would be a plain old slaughterhouse. He foresaw motorists on the Nimitz, catching a whiff of the manure, saying, "Oh, the bullshit from the *Mercury News*."

The rock 'em–sock 'em campaign Joe undertook to scuttle the Swift plant remains unique in my 40-year experience on the San Jose papers. No holds were barred; no quarter was given; none was asked. Our readers quickly discovered what we were up to, and most of them overwhelmingly approved. It may have been the most popular crusade our papers ever ran. Ken Conn was calling me home from Los Angeles to take over.

"You have a homeowners' group out there in Rosemary Gardens, don't you," he asked me.

We didn't, but I sensed I was being drafted. I replied, "I think you and I just founded one, and I'm stuck with being president."

At that point, though, I was still in the dark about certain happenings in my home office that had led Conn to summons me from L.A. as a matter of urgency. Back in San Jose a few days later I would find out about them in a disconcerting way.

In declaring war on Swift, Ridder was breaking with his longtime allies at City Hall. Since his arrival in San Jose as publisher 14 years earlier, Joe had been the staunch partner of City Manager A.P. "Dutch" Hamann in civic boosterism, notably in promoting the city's expansionist policy. As a team they had led the drive that was transforming San Jose from small town to metropolis, luring new people, commerce and industry, and annexing everything in sight from foothills to foothills and from the Bay to Morgan Hill. Now, for the first and probably only time, Ridder was preparing to fight City Hall.

He knew where to turn for counsel; he picked up the phone and called the late John Burnett, a San Jose lawyer. Their association in the anti-Swift war would be an ironic "strange bedfellows" alliance.

Burnett, great-grandson of California's first state governor Peter Burnett, was normally the bane of Ridder, Hamann *et al.* Fighting City Hall was his specialty. If you wanted to block an annexation, a rezoning, or a use permit, he was the lawyer you hired. A huge man with a gravelly voice that could rise to a roar on command, he knew every jot and tittle of the laws governing such matters, and how to use them to throw up roadblocks. Now he was Joe Ridder's attorney.

For tactical reasons, however, Ridder was reluctant to claim him. Joe's strategy was to keep a low profile, and to fight off the meat industry as an envi-

ronmental crusade for the whole community, not mentioning his concern about having a slaughterhouse right across the freeway from the newspapers' new headquarters.

The first skirmish of the war, I learned on returning to San Jose, was to take place before the county water commission, which had to OK the meat plant because it would be a large-volume water user and sewage producer. A public hearing was required, and I was sent to cover it. As I entered the room, I spotted Burnett's hulking form in a front row seat. Studiously ignoring him, I took my own seat at the press table, notebook in hand, with no foreboding of the quagmire I was about to be pushed into. The proceedings were routine, even dull, until opposition witnesses were called upon, and Burnett ponderously rose. What happened next was dismaying, especially to me.

"Mr. Chairman," Burnett announced, "I am here representing Mr. Harry Farrell, president of the Rosemary Gardens Homeowners Association."

This was my first tipoff that the "homeowner's group" Ken Conn and I had bantered about on the telephone had been accorded formal status, at least in my newspapers' scheme of things, and Burnett had been retained in *my name*. I hoped no one expected me to pay his bill.

Embarrassment at my immediate predicament overpowered that worry, however. Ostensibly I was in the room as an unbiased reporter, but I had been trapped unawares in gross conflict of interest. I buried my face deep in my notebook while Burnett— "my lawyer"—inveighed sonorously and at length against the evils of Swift's proposal. When the hearing mercifully ended, I raced for my office to find out what the hell was going on.

What had happened was that Burnett had foreseen a problem with Ridder's desire to remain behind the scenes in fighting the meat company. For legal, ethical, or procedural reasons (I forget which) Burnett needed a *client of record* in whatever appearances he made; he could not represent an anonymity. So after Conn's phone call to me, I was it. Burnett had given my editors the impression that this was just a technicality; no one had dreamed he would spill the beans.

One thing was painfully obvious; if we were going to wage a quasi-military operation, we needed to tighten up our tactical liaison. Our lower echelons, notably the city desk which had sent me to cover the water commission, had been kept in the dark about how I had been compromised by the machinations of our general headquarters, the front office.

Once the trauma of exposure wore off, I was not too unhappy. As a Rosemary Gardens homeowner, I was indeed fearful of having a slaughterhouse upwind from me. So while my professional image had been battered a little, I was personally unwounded. My heart was in the anti-Swift war as much as Joe Ridder's was.

In our chagrin, we considered what to do next. Finally I offered a suggestion: Since my counterfeit homeowners' association had been held up to public view, why not legitimatize it?

So I went home and called in six or seven of my neighbors, who were as worried as I about the Swift plant, and belatedly the organization came into being in my den. We drew up an anti-Swift petition and obtained some 300 signatures on it in three or four hours of door-to-door canvassing. A story about the petition, under an eight-column banner in the *News*, started the ball rolling among similar neighborhood groups all over town. Soon thousands of names protesting the meat packing plant were on file. Violating a long-standing policy against running phone numbers in news stories, our papers happily printed the number of anyone circulating a petition.

At that point a decision was reached that I would have full charge of the Swift story, but because of my conflict of interest, my byline would be withheld. My first decision, when I got these marching orders, was to call a spade a spade. I banned the phrase "meat packing plant," which in my mind evoked tasty cold cuts. From then on we invariably referred to the proposed facility as a "slaughterhouse." I studied the semantics of the meat business, too, so that I could graphically describe the problems in disposing of "paunch manure" and "inedible offal." The latter, I explained to readers at every opportunity, included "intestines, hooves, eyeballs, abscessed livers, bones, horns, and the like."

The publisher himself added one creative touch to our coverage. The *Mercury* then ran "Today's Chuckle" regularly on the front page. For a time it was replaced by "Today's Swiftie": " 'We intend to slaughter only beef,' Tom Swift said sheepishly." This sort of thing was catching; one church announced its sermon as "A Swift Wind Bloweth No Man Good."

Then came my adventure in Grand Island, Nebraska, where Swift had its newest slaughterhouse—a fine, landscaped plant, the pride of its empire. It was "totally unobjectionable," the company claimed, and the San Jose plant would be a copy. Plans were laid by Swift and its boosters to take a delegation of San Jose councilmen, civic leaders, and media representatives to Grand Island to inspect the facility. The idea was that they would be flown into town for a fine dinner, given a tour of the plant first thing next morning when it was newly washed down, and then whisked away to a two-martini lunch at a country club. They would presumably return to San Jose with rave reviews.

A week before this scheduled junket, I was quietly dispatched to Grand Island to reconnoiter. I checked into a motel, announcing myself to no one, and started ringing doorbells in residential neighborhoods near the slaughterhouse. Some of the people I called on worked there and were happy with it, but many were unhappy, too. There had been a bitter zoning battle when the plant had gone in, I learned, and the sore losers were only too happy to sign statements for me, denouncing it.

I was well prepared to sabotage Swift's P.R. junket when the San Jose delegation arrived three or four days later. I took the group by surprise and was waiting at the bottom of the ramp when its plane landed in late afternoon at the bleak Grand Island airport. It included several of my reporter friends from competitive media—San Jose's neighborhood weeklies and radio and TV stations. Graciously I offered to haul them around town in my Hertz car. By now they were vaguely uncomfortable about the Swift story and concerned for their reportorial integrity, knowing their trip was subsidized by one of the parties at interest. They wanted to get away from their keepers and do some sniffing around on their own. Could I take them to talk to some citizens-at-large? "Happy to," I said.

By now I had every Swift hater in town staked out. I drove my colleagues around for a while, pointed to a house in a random way, and said, "Let's try this one." My friends rang the doorbell, encountered a woman I had talked to the previous day, and kept their pencils, microphones, tape recorders, and cameras going while she said (as I knew she would), "That slaughterhouse is the stinkingest thing I ever lived next to!" My next stop was at a farmhouse I had visited earlier, where the occupant said, "Don't let anyone tell you there's no smell. You'd swear you'd never eat meat again in your life!"

That kind of talk, fed back to San Jose on the evening TV news and the radio, and in the neighborhood papers, had enormous impact.

I had one confederate in the visiting San Jose delegation. Because representatives of all media had been invited, its pro-Swift organizers had had to ask someone from our papers also, though we were clearly "the enemy." Paul Conroy, managing editor of the *News*, was therefore along. Late on the night the group arrived, Paul and I rendezvoused in his motel room to map strategy for turning the next morning's tour of the Swift plant into a public relations fiasco.

I had taken my own tour earlier in the week, presenting myself unannounced after dropping my cloak of anonymity. Graciously, the slaughterhouse executives had shown me everything. The really sickening smells, I had discovered, emanated from the rendering room. I knew the Swift people would hurry the touring group through that part of the plant (as they'd tried to do with me) and on to the spotless, odorless cold storage areas. So I told Paul, "When you get to the rendering room, stall as long as you can. Ask every question you can think of, to keep everyone there as long as possible. They won't be able to take it for long."

The rendering room, where the "inedible offal" was reduced to tallow, looked a lot like a ship's engine room. The ceiling was 20 or 30 feet high, and the upper regions were reached by steel ladders. On my own tour I had learned that convection currents carried the fetid air upward, so that near the ceiling the stench was unbearable. So I told Paul to request, for the delegation, an inspection of the higher elevations.

The next morning our plan worked to perfection. After a few minutes in the rendering room, several of the San Jose visitors began to sicken. When the late Councilman Robert Welch started his climb to the top, he turned a shade greener with every step of the ladder. Halfway up he turned back with acute nausea and rushed outside, refusing to complete the tour. He held an impromptu news conference on the spot, declaring, "As long as I'm on the council, no plant like this will *ever* be built in San Jose." The other reporters, of course, were taking down and taping every word for home consumption.

Back in San Jose the showdown on the slaughterhouse was fast approaching, with a hearing scheduled before the city planning commission, whose permit Swift needed. Before that, however, one more bizarre act remained to be played out at the *Mercury News*.

On a Saturday morning Joe Ridder and Ken Conn met with Swift's lawyer and Dutch Hamann, usually their crony, behind the closed doors of Joe's office. The city manager was still fronting for Swift; he wanted their plant badly for San Jose and still hoped to talk Ridder into going along with it.

Joe laid mischievous plans for the encounter. He had artist Dick Flood work up an editorial page cartoon, a vicious one by our standards then. It showed an ungainly cow labeled "Swift Slaughterhouse" lolling in a bathtub marked "San Francisco Bay." The murky water sloshing around the cow was labeled "Pollution." A cruelly caricatured Dutch Hamann (with a name tag to make sure everyone recognized him) was happily scrubbing the cow's back.

Ridder, who fought hard but never meanly, had no intention of running the cartoon under any circumstances. But Hamann didn't know that. Joe had Flood's drawing made up in zinc and a glossy proof

San Jose Mercury News
Dick Flood's cartoon never ran, but it did its job.

pulled. Both were lying amid the clutter on the publisher's desk, where the city manager couldn't miss them when he entered the office.

As further preparation for the meeting, Ridder had Conroy, managing editor Oscar Liden of the *Mercury*, and me sitting outside in the newsroom, apparently awaiting orders. Actually we were only window dressing, to convey the impression that Joe was ready to launch a meat-packing Armageddon in the Sunday paper unless Swift backed down.

The meeting in the publisher's office dragged on for hours, painfully for Paul and Oscar, who were executives called in on their day off, but pleasingly for me, a Guild member on overtime. What was said in Ridder's office that day I'm not sure, but I know that Joe, as host, poured a couple of rounds of drinks before a break for lunch (probably across the street at the old DeAnza Hotel). When the group reconvened in the afternoon more liquor was offered and Hamann partook, for when he emerged late in the day, the usually ebullient city manager was unsteady, disheveled, and beaten. He had tossed in Swift's towel. Joe summoned his chauffeur-driven Rolls Royce and had Hamann delivered safely home.

The formal denouement came a few days later in a packed city council chamber, at the planning commission's hearing on the slaughterhouse. After long and impassioned appearances by its foes, a Swift spokesman gracefully announced that the company, out of respect for the feelings of so many sincere if misled San Joseans, was withdrawing its application for the use permit. There was talk for awhile about relocating the proposed slaughterhouse in Gilroy, but that fizzled too. It finally went to Stockton.

At the time I almost felt sorry for the Swift people, who had been so decent through it all. But I have no long-term regrets. Our battle against the slaughterhouse was one of the first great environmental stands taken in San Jose. (The militant environmentalist movement was still several years in the future.)

Today the San Jose Foreign Trade Zone occupies a site close to the acres Swift would have filled with stockyards. *TV Guide* is printed nearby; Apple computers are assembled not far away. The area has generated not a few hundred jobs in animal killing, but many thousands in high tech.

Had Swift come in, other meat packers would have followed; one tried, in fact. San Jose's whole north side could have gone to slaughtering and noxious heavy industry, and our city today might be known not as the metropolis of Silicon Valley but as Omaha West.

CHAPTER XII
Young Man In A Hurry

A pleasant rogue, he tried to buy his ticket to immortality.
One of his mistakes was bidding too low.

William Penn Patrick, who flared cometlike across the California political firmament in the 1960s, was a young man in a hurry. As a shortcut to glory, he tried to buy the Republican Party—lock, stock, and elephant.

As things turned out, I had a hand in stopping him.

At 35, Patrick had scratched his way to a fortune manufacturing and marketing his Holiday Magic cosmetics. His operation, in San Rafael, worked on a pyramid principle: salesmen recruited salesmen who recruited more salesmen, and the money was passed up the line. It enabled Patrick, at the top, to proclaim himself (with characteristic modesty) a "self-made millionaire."

In 1966 he decided the time was ripe for a flier into another endeavor that fascinated him, politics. But this time he was determined not to scratch. For him there would be no struggling apprenticeship as councilman, supervisor, or mayor. He chose the governor's office as an appropriate starting place. He intended ultimately, he told his friends, to become president.

Patrick was singularly lacking in most resources deemed essential in politics. He had no base, no experience, no training, no name recognition. What he did have was an oversupply of gall and a lot of dough. The fact that the GOP already had two eminent seekers of the governorship, San Francisco Mayor George Christopher and an actor named Reagan, daunted him not.

I was on the politics beat then, and I recall when Patrick's first press release crossed my desk. There was nothing especially unusual about a total unknown announcing for governor; every election brings out its crop of oddballs and egomaniacs. Ordinarily such a long shot candidacy is a hand-to-mouth enterprise, its resources limited to a forlorn mimeograph machine on the candidate's kitchen table. Patrick's was different, however, with slick press handouts on red-white-and-blue, star-spangled stationery. And not long after his kickoff announcement, his hitherto anonymous face appeared on 500 expensive billboards from the Oregon line to the Mexican border.

From the word go, the Patrick campaign was a sizzler, as he gave his combative instincts free rein. He had grown up in North Carolina and was an early practitioner of the good-ol'-boy, corn pone rhetoric that would take Jimmy Carter into the White House a decade later. He scorned the party regulars. When someone told him he should "pay his dues" in grass roots spadework before shooting for the Number One spot, he purred, "People are tar'd of people who do precinct work, then get on central committees, and then run for little ol' things like the Assembly." He had nothing but contempt for his opponents: Pat Brown was a "fat slob," Reagan a "mental light-weight," Christopher a "dull plodder."

San Jose Mercury News

William Penn Patrick. He aimed high.

A rags-to-riches theme pervaded Patrick's literature. His campaign biography, prepared by a high-
priced Los Angeles public relations firm, related,
"For the first 15 years of his life, Patrick lived all the
frustrations, hopelessness, and degradation of
unending poverty. His day began at 4 A.M. and ended
at dark. His present and future were tied together in
bone-marrow fatigue."

When word of how he was maligning his origins
filtered east, an uproar ensued. Baxter Omohundro of
the *Mercury News* Washington Bureau went to
North Carolina and tracked down the candidate's
father, 72-year-old Dack Patrick, retired in apparent
affluence. Crusty old Dack flatly denied his son's tale
of deprivation.

"We had plenty," he boasted. "I had $20,000 in the
bank, a good contracting business, a farm, and business and rental property hereabouts. I always tried to
be a good daddy to Bill, but he was unruly and didn't
want to go to school. He ran away in 1946."

Omohundro's story broke, by chance, while Patrick
was campaigning in San Jose. I went to get his reaction before we printed it. His performance was a
classic of ruthlessness. One might imagine that

anyone in his shoes, however hard-shelled, would be
momentarily shaken if denounced as a fraud by his
own father. Not Patrick. He struck back like a cornered rattlesnake: "This forces me to come out and
attack my father. I have no choice."

One had to admire Patrick's sure-footedness. To
demean his father was sure to set the wrong way with
a lot of voters; so once he chose that tack, he had to
make Daddy look as bad as possible. How? Raise an
"other woman" specter.

"The old man, he's married to another woman, not
my mother," the candidate drawled. "Mother died
when I was 10, in childbirth. She was advised against
it, and something went wrong. I lived with my father
and stepmother for five years, and they treated me
like an animal."

As is now ancient history, Patrick scarcely made a
dent in the returns. Reagan won the Republican
gubernatorial primary (with 1,417,000 votes to
Christopher's 675,000 and Patrick's pitiful showing
of 40,000) and went on to beat the incumbent Pat
Brown in the fall.

After the primary, Patrick wasted no time on
regrets. His try for governor had really been a dry run
anyway. Now he began setting the stage for what he
probably had had in mind the whole time, a run for
U.S. senator. It was in pursuit of a Senate seat that he
embarked on his boldest, most grandiose venture.
Others might "buy" a lawmaker now and then;
Patrick set out to purchase a whole political party.

He moved slowly at first, and for a time that fall no
one caught on to what he was up to. The Reagan-
Brown runoff held everybody's attention; who was
paying heed to the vanquished make-up merchant
from Marin? However, I soon began to get strange little tips—hints that something funny was afoot. All I
could do with them, in the hurly-burly of the campaign, was file them away mentally. Actually, a
ferocious backstage battle had broken out within
the GOP.

A word is needed here about the structure of the
State Republican Party. The governing body is the
State Central Committee, which elects the party
officers. In 1966 the central committee consisted of
about a thousand members—principally the Republican nominees for all partisan offices (governor,
State Legislature, Congress, whatever) *plus three to
five other persons appointed by each of these
nominees according to a formula in the Election Code.*
The appointments were normally parceled out as
rewards to the nominees' friends and backers, with
the tacit understanding that they would follow their
sponsors when it came to voting on intra-party matters. Legally, however, they were free agents, and in
that Patrick saw his chance. If he could corral enough

renegade appointees, he could wrest control of the party from the Establishment.

In Churchill's phrase, Patrick struck at the GOP's soft underbelly. Throughout California there were certain congressional and legislative districts so solidly Democratic that the Republicans could not have won them if they had nominated Abraham Lincoln himself. Yet in each of these no-chance districts they felt compelled to "show the flag" with some sort of candidate, no matter how dismal his prospects. In recruiting such sacrificial lambs, party leaders played on their egos and their gambler instincts. The long-shot hope of an upset was always held out. What about campaign money? Why, the party would take care of that. But alas, when the chips were down, party funds were always steered into other races where there was more hope. Thus along about October, these dispirited candidates found themselves in tough, grinding, uphill contests—and broke. They were ripe for a proposition Patrick would put to them.

His plan for taking over the party had several parts. First he undertook to discredit the able, energetic incumbent state chairman, Dr. Gaylord Parkinson, a San Diego gynecologist (still remembered as the lawgiver who handed down the national GOP's Eleventh Commandment: "Thou shalt not speak ill of any Republican."). Parkinson was a firm Reagan ally, but Patrick incredibly denounced him as a "leftwinger." The attack so enraged Atherton multimillionaire Lee Kaiser, the party's finance chairman, that he fired off a letter to Patrick, "In my opinion, you are not only a dastard, but a *dirty* dastard."

The Republican leadership lived in fear that word of this dogfight would leak to the press during the fall campaign, shattering the party's fragile facade of unity and jeopardizing Reagan's chances. Incredibly, it did not. But with Reagan at last safe in victory, my sources in the party began pouring out the whole strange tale. What they told me was so grotesque that I decided to postpone a long-planned vacation to authenticate it. So the post-election week found me tracking down the "sacrificial lambs" now licking their wounds of defeat all over the state, to see if they would confirm the brazen approach which (I was hearing) Patrick had made to them. A couple of these losers were in the San Jose area, but I found a lot of them in places like Compton and Watts. They were more than ready to talk, and their stories were amazingly similar.

From candidate after candidate I heard how, when their money had dried up in the final campaign weeks, Patrick emissaries had visited them offering a flat-out deal. Money would be pumped into their flagging

campaigns if they would appoint to the state central committee whomever Patrick told them to. The going rate: $250 to $300 per seat.

In some cases a soft sell had been used, with the *quid pro quo* only hinted at. But one congressional candidate told me Patrick's people had used a "brute force approach."

Patrick might have had better luck if he hadn't tried to buy the appointments at cut-rate prices. One Assembly nominee in Compton told me he had needed $2,000 to mail out a brochure and would have sold two appointments for that much money. But the top offer was only $600; so he turned it down.

Who were the shock troops that made the offers? Almost without exception they were executives, distributors, or salesmen for Holiday Magic.

After a dozen interviews, I had the raw material for a five-part expose. Only one element was missing; I needed a response from Patrick himself. I put through a call to him in San Rafael and arranged to meet him at a bar in the Fairmont Hotel. Confronted with signed statements of the men he had tried to buy, he shook his head sadly and said, "Some of these fellows have no more integrity than a sponge."

Once again I had to admire his agility under pressure. Realizing I had a story that could mortally wound him, he moved instantly to take the edge off it by giving me a story of his own. There, in that dim-lit cocktail lounge, he "announced"—formally, unequivocally, and exclusively to me—that he would run against incumbent Republican Sen. Tom Kuchel in 1968. "Sen. Kuchel," he said, "is the biggest ass that ever hit the country."

Patrick still thought he could pull off his coup—seize the Republican machinery and install his own slate of officers so that the party would be under his thumb for his Senate campaign.

My articles, which ran in mid-November, let his cat out of the bag. With the approach of the state central committee's reorganization meeting in January, however, suspense remained. No one was sure how many delegates had taken Patrick up on his offer.

On the eve of the meeting, in Sacramento, he was still claiming firm commitments from at least 400 members. At a Patrick "hospitality room" in the El Mirador Hotel, hundreds of delegates were gorging themselves on a fabulous spread of fried chicken, rare roast beef, prawns, liver and bacon, *hors d'oeuvres*, and drinkables without limit.

It was all for nought. The next day in a showdown roll call, Patrick's power bid collapsed like a soggy souffle. Whatever mercenary troops he had purchased had deserted. A last-ditch call for a secret ballot, which might have stiffened his wilting ranks, was shouted down. The Reagan forces remained firmly in the driver's seat.

As the convention broke up, one Establishment leader who had gloated over my expose of Patrick's shenanigans, sidled up to me. "I guess now you'll hit him again, hey!" he said. Then in a whisper, "...but don't hit him too hard. We want him to come back and throw more of those great feeds!"

Patrick stuck it out for six more months as a nominal challenger to Kuchel before throwing in the towel in favor of the fiery, rightwing state superintendent of public instruction, Max Rafferty. Rafferty went on to defeat Kuchel in the 1968 GOP primary, only to be beaten that fall by Democrat Alan Cranston.

For several more years Patrick remained visible on the Republican scene. In 1971 he urged that Robert McNamara be tarred and feathered and that Earl Warren be hanged as a traitor. He took up a paramilitary hobby, collecting vintage aircraft.

On September 24, 1972, one of his planes, a F86 Sabre jet, crashed on takeoff at Sacramento, slamming into an ice cream parlor. The pilot escaped with broken bones and a cut face, but 22 persons on the ground, including 10 children, were killed.

Nine months later, Patrick took off at the controls of another old plane, a World War II P51 Mustang, to overfly a 6,000-acre ranch he had acquired in Lake County. Suddenly he went into a steep dive, crashing into a ravine.

He died instantly.

CHAPTER XIII
The Man Who Turned Around

In any cause, there is no zealot like the convert.
For one former revolutionary, the turnabout has been 180 degrees.

On the morning of May 2, 1967, I was in Sacramento covering the State Legislature. In the Assembly, floor debate rambled on tediously over trivialities; so as noon approached, I cut out for lunch. I got as far as the Capitol rotunda before I walked head-on into history in the making.

Entering through the front door of the building was a column of black men in black berets and black leather jackets, armed with rifles, carbines, shotguns, and pistols; they wore web cartrdige belts and were festooned with bandoliers. They marched silently, single file, at intervals like an infantry patrol. I had no idea who they were. I spotted another newsman, Van Shumway of UPI, trailing along behind them in bewilderment; so I fell in alongside him.

Purposefully the invaders made their way through the rotunda and down a corridor to an elevator, which disgorged them onto the second floor outside the Assembly. Without pause they pushed past the two middle-aged, civilian sergeants at arms who guarded the swinging gates to the chamber. Within seconds they were inside.

It was the first and only armed invasion of the Legislature in its 133-year history. It was also the opening of a new chapter in American militancy, sending out a shockwave that would ripple for a decade and making the nation indelibly aware of a new force, the Black Panthers. Until then the Panthers had been an insignificant band, virtually unknown outside Oakland.

A hectic hour ensued. Debate in the Assembly came to a standstill, amid angry shouting from the rostrum and the floor. The Panthers milled around or took seats in the VIP section. Ultimately, they let themselves be rounded up and taken to a State Police cubicle where they surrendered their loaded weapons to officers who removed the bullets. No gun had been discharged, and nothing that had happened could be called violent.

Finally, the nonplussed police returned the weapons to the invaders and let them go, finding no violation on which to book them. In the confusion, no one remembered an obscure section of the Government Code making it a misdemeanor to disrupt the Legislature in session. But when the Panthers regathered later at a nearby service station, 26 of them were arrested for a technical Fish and Game Code violation—carrying loaded weapons in a motor vehicle.

One of those taken into custody was Eldridge Cleaver.

In the Capitol pressrooms we spent the afternoon trying to put the story together. The Panthers, 54 of them altogether, had come from Oakland to demonstrate against a gun-control bill. The rhetoric had been bitter. Besides their firearms, the Panthers had brought to Sacramento a formal call for rebellion, signed by Huey Newton, which one of them had read in a loud voice in a Capitol corridor: "Toward people of color, the racist power structure of America has but one policy: repression, genocide, terror, and the Big Stick...The time has come for black people to arm themselves against this terror...The black community of America must rise up as one man to halt the progression of a trend that leads inevitably to their total destruction."

The lawmakers were stunned and outraged. Gov. Ronald Reagan, who was picnicking that noon on the Capitol lawn with a class of eighth graders from Pleasant Hill, missed a direct encounter with the Panthers, but later he issued a bitter condemnatory statement. Jitters set in throughout the Capitol, whose doors until then had seldom been locked, even at night. Reagan's security guard was beefed up.

Beginning that day, the Black Panthers would be the cutting edge of black militarism across the land. The life of Eldridge Cleaver, an outlaw since adolescence, would take the strangest turns of all.

A shoot-out with the Oakland police the following year left Cleaver wounded and another Panther dead. Cleaver, who had already spent more than a third of his life in San Quentin, Folson, and Soledad, was rearrested for parole violation. From a cell in Vacaville, denying all guilt and calling himself a "political prisoner," he gave vent to his wrath in a letter to the governor:

> Those who fastened the handcuffs to my wrists, the shackles around my legs, the chain around my body, put me into a car, transported me to this place, and turned me over to the keepers here were mere functionaries, automatons, carrying out their "duties" in Adolf Eichmann's spirit....
>
> The notorious, oppressive, racist, and brutal Oakland Police Department is at the heart of the matter. This gestapo force openly and flagrantly terrorizes the black people of Oakland...I've seen their murderous hatred burning in their eyes....On April 6, 1968, they attempted to murder me, shot me, and did murder a member of our party, Bobby Hutton, 17 years old. And then they charged me with attempting to murder them!...
>
> Are you outraged, governor?

Whether or not Reagan ever saw Cleaver's polemic, which ran to 13 pages, there was no direct answer. But a response of sorts came after Cleaver was released on a writ of *habeas corpus*, on $50,000 bail.

By now a hero of the left, he was invited to lecture on experimental sociology at U.C. Berkeley. Outraged, the governor moved in his capacity as a U.C. regent to deny academic credit for the course. Cleaver's fury erupted anew. In *Ramparts* magazine, he hurled a direct challenge to Reagan:

> You are a cowardly, craven-hearted wretch. You are not a man. You are a punk....I would like to have the opportunity to balance the books. Therefore, Mickey Mouse, I challenge you to a duel, to the death, and you can choose the weapons. And if you can't relate to that, right on. Walk, chicken, with your ass picked clean.

Cleaver's interval of freedom on bail was brief. The Court of Appeal reversed his *habeas corpus* and ordered him to report in 60 days for reincarceration. It was an order never honored. On the eve of his scheduled surrender he fled the country.

He now wore the cloak of a martyr, and his deeply introspective, best-selling autobiography, *Soul on Ice*, was making him an international celebrity. During a seven-year exile in Cuba, Algeria, and France he became a propaganda prize for international communism, wined, dined and wooed in capitals from Moscow to Peking, Havana to Hanoi. In Algeria he set up an international headquarters for the Black Panther party.

Then disillusionment set in. Suddenly Cleaver was fed up with being a fugitive. Through diplomatic channels he sent out the word that he wanted to come home and face the music.

I had kept track of him only in a desultory way over the years since I had witnessed his, and the Panthers', debut in Sacramento. I knew of his exile and of his return, supposedly as a penitent, but I was taken by surprise to learn in mid-1980 that he had quietly taken up residence in Cupertino.

Earlier that year Superior Court Judge Winton McKibben in Oakland had ordered him to perform, as the price for his final freedom, 2,000 hours of unpaid community service over a five-year period. He was working away at the obligation as an assistant in the De Anza College library.

My curiosity led me to seek him out, to hear his side of the experience we had shared, unknown to each other, in the legislative invasion 13 years earlier. So not long thereafter I sat down with him in a quiet library corner to reminisce. Not surprisingly his recollections differed markedly from mine.

The storming of the Legislature had seemed at the time, to its witnesses and to an outraged state and nation, an act of unmitigated outlawry. It was far

De Anza College librarian Eldridge Cleaver checks out some books.

San Jose Mercury News

from that, I learned from Cleaver. The Panthers had covered their legal bases in advance.

"We checked with a lawyer before we went," he told me. "So we had our guns in a legal manner. The law at the time said we could have live rounds in the magazine but not in the chamber. We didn't have any rounds in the chambers; so when they checked our guns, they had no grounds to confiscate them."

For his own part, Cleaver had taken additional precautions because he was on parole, only four months out of Soledad after nine years of a 14-year sentence.

"I didn't carry a weapon," he said, and I got permission from my parole officer to go, as a reporter for *Ramparts.*

"Did your parole officer know there would be guns?"

"No, I just told him I wanted to accompany a delegation that was going there to protest some pending legislation."

The attorney who briefed the Panthers, in advance of their foray, would become prominent politically. He was John George, later an Alameda County supervisor.

Cleaver's legal caution paid off. Photos of the raid clearly showed him weaponless; so of the 26 Panthers arrested, he was the only one released the same day on his own recognizance. Moreover, his parole was not revoked—not then. That would not happen until after the shoot-out the next year.

Comparing notes, Cleaver and I had differing though not conflicting memories of the instant the gun-wielding band had burst in on the started lawmakers.

My prime recollection was a vignette of the late Assemblyman Carlos Bee of Hayward, who was presiding as speaker pro tem. By the time the Panthers had reached the Assembly chamber, a TV crew had picked up their trail. The nearsighted Bee, at the rostrum some 80 feet from the Panthers' point of entry in the rear, spotted only the bulky camera, not the guns. Mindful of the Legislature's then-ironclad rule against cameras on the floor, Bee vented his first wrath on the television men: "Sergeant at arms, get those photographers out of here!" A considerable time elapsed before he realized who the real invaders were.

Cleaver's memory of the same moment focused not on the rostrum, but on the floor, as the legislators turned to see what the commotion was about.

"I remember Assemblyman Willie Brown," he said. "Willie knew us, he recognized us, and his eyes were as big as saucers."

The time Cleaver had served, before the raid on the Legislature, was for six counts of rape and assault—three counts with intent to commit murder and three with a deadly weapon.

"Were you guilty?" I asked him that afternoon in the library.

His response was in stark contradiction to his earlier defiant denials: "Yeah, I was guilty. I have never been sent to prison for something I didn't do."

Inevitably, with the 1980 presidential election only two months away, our discussion drifted toward politics. That was when the totality of Cleaver's turnabout struck me.

He casually remarked that he was supporting his old enemy, Ronald Reagan.

"Why?"

"I think we need a strong person in there."

With that, Cleaver launched into a monologue on the essentiality of a powerful federal establishment.

"The United States of America cannot stand four more years of Jimmy Carter," he said. "In exile I had a good chance to look at the communist world strategy and their *modus operandi*, which is really what turned me around and opened my eyes. The people of the Third World and Europe and the communist countries see American capitalism as being on its deathbed. They feel we're paralyzed and cannot react to or cope with their thrust for power... And looking at the way Jimmy Carter has handled the international situation, and Zbigniew Brzezinski, who's calling the shots, I think they've caused a series of disasters that will not allow the United States to do its job in competing with the Soviet Union... It's true that the capitalist system is in a lot of trouble, but our economy has evolved from an agrarian base into the highest technological society, and it was done under the republican form—the democratic form—of government that we have here, and this is something very precious."

Strange words for one who once proclaimed his "seething hatred of all governments."

In any cause, there is no zealot like the convert. Cleaver, having left the radical movement, has swung all the way across the spectrum:

—Where he once demanded exemption of all blacks from military service, he is now an outspoken advocate of the draft.

—Where he was once an outlaw, he now favors the death penalty not only for homicide but for any violent, aggravated assault. To those who argue that it is not a deterrent, he says, "That's a big lie. Nothing makes me move like death makes me move."

—Where he once ranted about "flagrant and indefensible" invasion of his rights, he now crusades for what is anathema to civil libertarians, a national I.D. card.

"We have a real need to control the comings and goings in this country," he told a 1981 audience at San Jose State University. He said "thousands and thousands" of communist agents had filtered into the United States, noting that while he was a fugitive, he found it easy to slip in and out of the country undetected.

Since our first meeting in the De Anza library, Eldridge and I have talked a lot, over ravioli, clam chowder, and a margarita or two. Just after Reagan had been elected, I was curious about the feedback Cleaver had generated by endorsing him. Eldridge had predicted, when I first disclosed the endorsement in my column, that his old enemy Reagan would not welcome it.

Not so, it had turned out. The Reagan people had sent a staff man up from Los Angeles to talk to Cleaver, who had ended up making some radio spots for them.

"Did you catch any flak?" I asked him.

"Only from people like Ron Dellums. Ron went around telling people I was crazy."

From Reagan, our conversation turned to Jerry Brown.

"I think he has a lot of secret life going on," Eldridge said. "Usually with a governor, you know what he does, where he goes, and so forth, and I think the people have a right to know those things. But Governor Brown, I think, goes to great lengths to maintain a certain secrecy, and as a result his administration suffers. In California we expect greatness in our governors, you know. We don't like them just to stumble along and make it without distinguishing themselves in one way or the other. I think California's going to have an inordinate influence on the whole country. It's unheard-of that after Nixon was disgraced in office, another Californian is able to come along and become president. California people are different. There's a different kind of thing going on out here, that's not tied to tradition the way the rest of the country is. I refer to Californians as the frontier people."

Early in 1981 Eldridge got excited about a project that would help fulfill his public service obligation, which by then he had whittled to about 1,400 hours. Working with students from the De Anza, Foothill, West Valley, San Jose State, and Santa Clara University campuses, he was organizing a Fourth of July program for San Jose. He was really fired up, declaring, "It's going to be a pro-democracy, pro-American thing. We want to get a combined high school band, and we're trying to get someone like Bob Dylan to come in to provide special music. We're going to have an American Indian, a Chicano, a black, an Irishman, Italian, Anglo-Saxon. We want to get the whole melting pot and really bury the hatchet on the past.''

And that was to be only the beginning. "We want to start a Fourth of July Movement," he said, "to take this message to the college campuses around the country and offer some opposition to the organizations that are now there spreading Marxist ideas, communist ideas, and other philosophies. Every kind of group is out there trying to recruit people, but there's no real force sticking up for America in a meaningful way."

An Independence Day event at San Jose State did, in fact, evolve from Cleaver's project, though not on the grand scale of his dreams.

Whatever Eldridge Cleaver feels at any given time, he gives voice to it with intensity. By early fall of 1981, other matters were on his mind.

He had tentatively embraced Mormonism, undismayed that the priesthood of Latter-day Saints had until two years earlier been closed to blacks.

"The Mormons weren't the ones who owned the slaves," he told me. "The Methodists, Baptists, Presbyterians, Episcopalians, Catholics—they owned the slaves. The Mormons were fighting for their lives too, you know."

And, Cleaver was planning to run for mayor of Oakland if he could recall the black incumbent Lionel Wilson, who as a judge had once sentenced him to prison.

"Crime is rampant," he raged. "We need a program to improve relationships with the police and really deal with the behavior of a lot of young people." (This from a man who had once seethed at the Oakland police as "bloodthirsty troops...an occupying army ...an evil force with its sword of terror thrust into the heart of the black community.")

"Since you've turned conservative," I asked him, "are you called an Uncle Tom?"

"Yeah, by a few people," he said, "but it doesn't work out, not with me, because you're either a Tom or you're not, right?....

"You know what happens to radicals? When they see something in society they think is wrong, they buy the opposition's propaganda. The opposition tries to make the *status quo* look as though it were ordained by God and supported by the Constitution,

Wide World Photos

At the State Capitol, May 2, 1967—the "dart board" photo: The author, center, stares straight into the camera from between black-bereted Eldridge Cleaver (dark glasses) and Bobby Seale. To the right of Seale, in light felt hat, is Bobby Hutton, later killed in the Oakland police shoot-out that brought about Cleaver's reincarceration.

and therefore, if you try to change anything, you're overthrowing the government. So then the radicals say, 'OK, if that's what we have to do, then we'll overthrow the government.' Well, I've changed from that view. I used to be mad about *everything*. Now there are only certain things I'm mad about.''

When I had prepared for my first meeting with Eldridge, the one in the De Anza library, I had dug out our 1967 clippings on the Black Panthers' tumultuous debut before the Legislature. Because I had followed them every step of the way, I was in almost every picture that had been taken that day. One AP photo showed four Panthers arguing with a State Police officer; in background center, between Cleaver and Bobby Seale and staring straight into the camera, was Farrell.

Eldridge studied this picture at length with an ambigious, reflective look. Then he started to laugh.

"I've been carrying you around with me for a long time," he said.

I was puzzled.

"You see," he explained, "the Black Panther Party made a poster out of this picture. I had it blown up really big, about three feet tall. It was on my wall all the time I was in Algeria. I was looking at your face all those years."

"Who did you think I was?"

"I thought you were a cop. We used you for a dart board."

"How did that work?"

"It worked just fine, you know—just fine!"

CHAPTER XIV
A Matter Of Conscience

"Military necessity" was the reason given for interning the West Coast Japanese after Pearl Harbor. Then why did they wait till the danger had passed?

Four decades after Pearl Harbor, the World War II roundup and incarceration of 110,000 West Coast Japanese—Issei and Nisei alike—remains a tender spot on the American conscience. It is especially so for Californians who witnessed it, whether as victims, advocates, perpetrators, beneficiaries, or merely persons who acquiesced.

Such a trampling of the Bill of Rights is unthinkable today—or is it? Massive internment of Iranians in America was widely advocated during the 1979-81 hostage crisis.

The pretext for the evacuation of the Japanese in the spring of 1942, from the coastal zone to 10 stockades spread from Idaho to Arkansas, was military necessity. In a cavalier override of pertinent distinctions—loyalty or disloyalty, innocence or guilt—Gen. John L. DeWitt, the West Coast Army commander, told the House Naval Affairs Subcommittee, "A Jap's a Jap. It makes no difference whether he is an American citizen. You can't change him by giving him a piece of paper."

Grotesque perversions of logic characterized the public declarations of the time. Some two months after the United States entered the war, DeWitt said, "The very fact that no sabotage has taken place to date is a disturbing and confirming indication that such action will be taken."

Such contortions were not limited to the military mind. California's State Attorney General Earl Warren, who would soon become governor and later chief justice of the United States, echoed the general, testifying:

> The only reason we haven't had a disaster in California is that it is timed for a different date...Our day of reckoning is bound to come...I want to say the consensus among the law enforcement officers of this state is that there is more potential danger among the group of Japanese who were born in this country than from the alien Japanese who were born in Japan.

Even the astute Walter Lippmann, about the same time, was writing about the "sinister lack of sabotage on the West Coast."

The true motivations for the Japanese relocation were mixed. Gen. DeWitt, for his part, may actually have *believed* what he said about military need. He could scarcely be blamed for declaring, "I am not going to be a second Gen. Short," referring to the commander who had been removed for "dereliction of duty" at Pearl Harbor. Others, however, were moved by fear, bigotry, hatred, and greed. Sentiment was whipped up by rabble-rousers. Columnist Henry McLemore wrote, "Herd 'em up, pack 'em off, and give them the inside room of the badlands. Let 'em be pinched, hurt, hungry, and dead up against it.''

In the tenor of the time, the fact that they had done no wrong hardly mattered.

This shoddy chapter of history has returned to the headlines with an activist faction of Nisei stepping up pressures on Congress for redress. They seek $25,000 in damages, as belated national atonement for the incarceration of each individual, living or dead. The overall cost to the national treasury would run close to $3 billion.

Early in the debate over this plan, then-U.S. Sen. Sam Hayakawa visited the *Mercury News*. He denounced the restitution idea as ''ridiculous.'' That a senator of Japanese extraction should take that view was not surprising in itself. Within the overall Nisei community the redress proposal is highly controversial, many feeling that after so long a time, it could not importantly serve the cause of justice.

What was unsettling in Hayakawa's position was that he defended the relocation itself. The camps hadn't been so bad, he told us. Many Japanese farmers, who hadn't had a day's rest in 30 years, had had a three-year vacation. And there had been a ''huge revival of Japanese art'' in the camps. Moreover, asserted Hayakawa (who had never been interned, having spent the war teaching in Chicago), it had indeed been *necessary* to remove the Japanese from the coast, both for their own safety and the reassurance of those who feared them. The senator painted a grim picture of conditions in California at the time of the roundup.

''Absolute terror struck the West Coast,'' he said. ''There were blackouts every night from San Diego all the way up the coast. And we never knew when a Japanese submarine would come into San Francisco Bay.''

The next time I sat down to write a column, I could not let the senator's depiction go unchallenged.

I had been here during the time he spoke of; he had not. This was one case in which Hayakawa, who was often right, simply didn't know whereof he spoke. Not only were his facts askew; he was imprecise in his language, a grave lapse for one who first won acclaim as a semanticist.

During the first week or two after Pearl Harbor, there was much excitement and nervousness in San Jose, to be sure—and yes, some fear. But there was nothing close to the overpowering, pit-of-the-stomach fear implied by Hayakawa's phrase ''absolute terror.''

The schools stayed open. We never did have nightly blackouts; in the entire first week after Pearl Harbor, San Jose had only two, and there were probably no more than six or eight altogether, all after ''unidentified planes'' were reported. It was never confirmed

that the planes were Japanese; if they were, they left without dropping their bombs. The only direct, overt actions ever taken by Japanese forces against the American mainland came later, when on three occasions submarines lobbed a few shells onto beaches near Santa Barbara and in the Northwest.

Nor was there ever any need, as Hayakawa argued, to evacuate the Japanese for their own safety. Undeniably, Pearl Harbor brought a surge of ill will against them, compounded by suspicion and fear, but voices of good will were heard from the start, both within the Japanese community and the Caucasian establishment. Less than 24 hours after the bombs fell on Pearl, the secretary of San Jose's Japanese Association, J.S. Hirano, unequivocally denounced the attack. ''We consider ourselves Americans,'' he said. ''This is our country. We are anxious to show our loyalty to the United States.''

The following day the *Mercury Herald* editorialized:

> It is no time for hysterics, and it is noteworthy that with very few exceptions, citizens of Santa Clara County are cool...It does not make you a better American to toss an epithet at any person who looks like a Japanese. The presumption, if you see them, is that they are as good Americans as you are.

These were the things I told in the column I wrote after Hayakawa's visit. Some of the response was hostile. I had letters and phone calls berating me for ''opening old wounds.'' A Santa Cruz woman, brushing aside the premise that punishment should be only for the guilty, wrote, ''When I think of all those sailors lying at the bottom of Pearl Harbor or in Punch Bowl National Cemetery, I don't feel the California Japanese have any reasons for complaint.''

An argumentative reader in Morgan Hill told me, ''After the Japs pulled their sneak attack, don't you ever believe that all Japanese in this country were not in danger. And if they had not been all interned, how easy it would have been to have planted a few bad ones with the good ones, and all defense plants would have been easy prey for the black-hearted rascals. What I mean is, blood is thicker than water.''

That flew in the face of history, ignoring the fact that in other parts of the United States thousands of Japanese (including Hayakawa) remained at large throughout the war without incident. They included 160,000 in Hawaii, undeniably a war zone. It also ignored the rigid bureaucratic callousness with which the evacuation order was enforced. At a Maryknoll orphanage in Los Angeles, a priest told Army authorities that some of the children were only one-quarter Japanese, or less. The colonel in charge of the internment replied, ''If they have one drop of Japanese

In San Jose State College gym, Japanese-Americans register for relocation, early 1942.

blood in them, they go to camp." Moreover, if "blood is thicker than water," why weren't Italians and Germans rounded up, too?

By one reader, I was reminded that in 1941 even American-born Japanese had dual citizenship and thus owed allegiance to Hirohito. In some cases, this was true in a legalistic, technical sense, but it skirted the fact that the U.S. law of the time barred their Issei parents from American citizenship; in California, the Japanese-born couldn't even own real estate.

Joining the debate was a former San Jose mayor, Louis Solari, who shortly after Pearl Harbor had been a military intelligence officer in San Francisco. He contributed a footnote to history:

> I shall never forget that fateful midnight hour while on duty, February, 1942. A flash came across the communication panel reading, "Japanese fleet sailing toward the Pacific Coast." I immediately awakened Gen. DeWitt. When informed of the situation, he said, "Oh, my God, what shall I do?"

Then, according to Solari, after he and the general had prayed together, DeWitt "ordered the removal of the Japanese population from the West Coast, not because of disloyalty or possible sabotage, but for their personal protection and safety." Not only was this at odds with DeWitt's public stance at the time ("a Jap's a Jap"), but it failed to refute the main point of the column I had written: If the Japanese had been shipped out in the scare right after December 7, the action might have been militarily defensible, though still unconstitutional. In the first days of confusion, no one really knew who stood where—and even Abraham Lincoln had suspended *habeas corpus* in wartime.

The fact remains, however, that the vast majority of Issei and Nisei were permitted to live and work here until late spring. President Franklin Roosevelt did not issue the famous (or infamous) Executive Order 9066, which authorized the evacuation, until February 10. And few of the West Coast Japanese were shipped out until April or May. By then the scare was over; the blackouts were long past; the security threat, if there had ever been one, was contained. The feared invasion fleet had never arrived, and the feared sabotage had never come.

At San Jose High School that spring of 1942, there

were a score of Nisei in the graduating class, of which I was also a member. Many were honor students. They came to school daily without incident until a few weeks before the mid-June commencement; then they were put aboard the trains and taken from us. They got their diplomas later by mail.

If Gen. DeWitt truly believed the presence of the Japanese a threat to his command in February, why did he let them stay around until May?

On balance, only a small part of the response to my column was from carpers. Most readers who wrote me, especially non-Nisei, dwelt on poignant memories. Sid Burkett wrote of shipping out to Hawaii as a merchant seaman in June, 1942, and being amazed by what he found there:

> We were given stringent orders about being careful not to stray about. After all this was Pearl Harbor, full of secrets. Imagine my surprise when the first guard I saw as I came down the gangplank was a Japanese-American in a U.S. uniform, with a gun. When the tram came, it was driven by a Japanese-American. In fact, there were Japanese-Americans all over the place working on battleships, destroyers, and other paraphernalia of war. On the mainland they were "the enemy"; in Hawaii they were helping us win the war.

Of the mixed motivations for the internment of the Japanese, the most despicable was greed: the chance exploited by some to buy up their belongings or to grab their homes and farms (often held in the names of native-born children) at pennies on the dollar. Reader Armand Rynhard of Santa Cruz looked back on such gross conduct from an unusual perspective:

> I was at that very same time a refugee from Europe, run over by Hitler's juggernaut, and I knew of many cases where fine citizens had been denounced to the invading Nazis as being Jews by some greedy individuals who could get their hands on the belongings they left behind when they were "relocated."

I was taking a citizen-education class at Hollywood High. I was shocked to hear some people boast of their bountiful ransack exploits and openly and boisterously plan new sorties. We had a lovely Nisei neighbor, and the girl gave us a couple of fine antiques before leaving, knowing she would never find them later. It seems impossible to evaluate the total amount these people lost, stolen from them by greedy ransackers under the pretense of nationalistic fervor.

For Joan Benedetti, my column recalled a wrenching childhood experience in Irvington, now part of Fremont:

> What stands out in my mind, still vividly, is the day I came to school and all the Japanese children, our playmates and friends, were gone. The cross street in front of our school seemed empty without the handsome and friendly face of the eighth grade boy who had been the traffic patrol captain. Many of us cried throughout the day. I didn't understand it then and I don't now.

A letter from Diane Knaefler in Sunnyvale, who in 1942 had been a youngster in the San Gabriel Valley, may have best expressed the shame and outrage still smouldering within many Californians:

> My father had acquired many Japanese friends. Our family went into Los Angeles to see Mr. Fukui the night before he and his family were to be relocated. I remember my father saying to him, "They can't do this, not to you," and Mr. Fukui replying, "Otto, they can and they are. Why can't you accept it? If this is what my country needs, then I must do it."
>
> They had known each other so many years; Mr. Fukui and my father had fought side by side in the trenches in World War I under Gen. Pershing....
>
> On the way home I remember feeling very dead inside, and even after all these years just thinking about that night has the old wound bleeding pretty deeply. How can something that happened so long ago still bring such pain and distress?

CHAPTER XV
Earthquake Country

It's the imported Californians in whom earth tremors strike terror.
When the shaking starts, the natives just shrug—even after Coalinga.

When Sally Reed got her chance in 1981 to change jobs, moving from a second echelon berth at City Hall to the exalted post of county executive, she had to think about the pros and cons.

One of the cons in her mind, as she gazed from City Hall to the county's rust-and-glass tower a stone's throw away in the Civic Center, was earthquakes. The county executive's office, she knew, was on the eleventh floor of that less-than-reassuring high-rise where hardly anything had worked right since the day it opened. In a good shake, Sally wondered, how much would it sway up there? Finally the tugs of higher salary and challenge overrode her fears and she took the job in spite of them.

Later the same year, when I polled a number of persons about the five best and five worst things in San Jose, earthquakes were high on the "worst" lists of both County Executive Reed and Mayor Janet Gray Hayes. Nobody else even mentioned them.

That figured. Sally had grown up in Rolla, Missouri, and Janet Gray in Rushville, Indiana. It is those from afar in whom earthquakes strike dread. Native Californians (who would be terrified in a Midwest tornado or a Gulf hurricane) are fatalistic about them, even contemptuous.

Indeed we live beneath a seismic Sword of Damocles; everyone knows that. And no matter how hard we try, we are never prepared when it falls. The Coalinga quake of 1983 proved that.

A state geologist in Sacramento, John F. Davis, has written a chiling scenario for an earthquake equal to San Francisco's 1906 disaster, and he insists it is "absolutely inevitable." The Bayshore Freeway will be shut down for at least three days with collapsed overpasses; San Francisco and Oakland Airports and Moffett Field will be out of commission; the Dumbarton, San Mateo, San Francisco-Oakland, and Golden Gate Bridges will all be closed. Santa Clara Valley towns, built on silt, clay, and gravel washed down from the hills, will be harder hit than anywhere else.

Yet when Davis issued this grim prediction, early in 1982, old-timers from San Jose to Hollister just shrugged. They had felt the earth heave, heard the dishes rattle, watched the chandeliers swing, and restacked the groceries too often to get excited.

Nonetheless, seismology holds an acute fascination for those who dwell in Santa Clara Valley, the heart of earthquake country. It is ingrained in their culture. They know their sub-strata are traversed by the San Andreas, Calaveras, and Hayward Faults, and no one knows how many offshoots.

If politics make strange bedfellows, in San Jose earthquakes make good politics. It is not happenstance that the legislator who "wrote the book" of California earthquake law, including a requirement for fault-line disclosure in real estate reports, is State Sen. Alfred E. Alquist of San Jose. He pounced on the issue after 64 persons were killed in the San Fernando Valley earthquake of 1971. He dashed all over the state with his seismic safety subcommittee, reaping a bountiful publicity harvest. (In the process he gave a leg-up to another aspiring Santa Clara County politician; his consultant for the earthquake investigation was supervisor-to-be Rod Diridon.)

Nor is it coincidence that the county has given rise to two of the nation's best-known earthquake prognosticators, seeress Clarisa Bernhardt, known as the "Earthquake Lady," and County Geologist James Berkland. Clarisa, a regular in the *National Enquirer's* stable of psychics, foretells tremors by auras, vibrations, and visions. Berkland predicts them by his "seismic window theory," involving the alignment of earth, sun and moon. He publishes an annual forecast, catchily titled "Syzygy, Perigee, and Seismicity." Both Bernhardt and Berkland have fair records of being able to say, "I told you so."

Clarisa scored her first bull's-eye two days before Thanksgiving in 1974, when she told listeners to Los Gatos' tiny FM station, KRVE, that a 5.2 Richter quake would rock Hollister at 3 o'clock on Thanksgiving afternoon, causing major damage. If KRVE's weak line-of-sight signal ever reached Hollister, it certainly elicited nothing more than a yawn. Hollister wasn't called the Earthquake Capital for nothing; folks there could count on a jolt every time the San Andreas Fault slipped a little. Anyone trying to make a name as a quake forecaster could hardly miss with Hollister.

But two days later Clarisa's prediction was filled with uncanny precision. She hit the epicenter and the Richter rating on the nose, and she was only one minute off on the time. The 5.2 jolt at 3:01 was a doozy that struck fear even into the stout hearts of Hollister old-timers.

In the mid-1970s Clarisa stuck her neck out with repeated predictions of a cataclysm to come on March 8, 1978. The "Palmdale Bubble" of the San Andreas Fault would crack wide open, she said, starting a total rearrangement of Southern California. Over the ensuing 15 to 20 years all the valleys would sink into the sea, converting Los Angeles and San Diego into islands and Phoenix into a seaport. Dry land would rise in the Pacific, enabling mainlanders to drive to Hawaii.

As the critical date neared, Clarisa grew understandably nervous. *Something* had to happen on March 8 or her credibility would be shot. Or would it? She began to cover her bases by proclaiming that good thoughts, directed to any point on earth, could prevent or diminish any quake that might otherwise be catastrophic. Then she had a bronze medallion cast, with the inscription, "To Help Stop Earth-

quakes, Send Love to Our Planet." She began passing them out everywhere.

Thus Clarisa had it both ways. If there was a shake in Southern California on the appointed date, she had predicted it. If there wasn't, her medals had prevented it.

In the end things came out beautifully for her. Early on the morning of March 8, the newswires moved a paragraph about a tiny tremor in Anaheim. It was a little above 3 on the Richter scale—just enough to be felt without hurting anyone. With the wire story in hand, I called Clarisa.

"Well, you've got your quake," I told her.

She was thrilled. Her phone began ringing off the wall with calls from the Washington *Post*, the Baltimore *Sun*, the Melbourne, Australia, *Herald*, and TV and radio stations everywhere. A Hamburg, Germany, magazine writer called requesting an interview.

"The nicest thing of all," Clarisa said later, "was that the quake happened early in the morning. I didn't have to worry the rest of the day. I thought it was very accommodating."

She still insists that the little Anaheim shake was only the overture, and that the massive geographical revision she predicted still lies ahead. Every jolt we feel furthers the process, she says.

One of my readers with more than ordinary respect for Clarisa's Palmdale Bubble prediction was Linda Weinstein. She called me the day before the bubble was supposed to burst, to report that her cat, Mazel, "was hyperactive last night, biting its tail and everything. And usually Mazel's a very calm cat."

The "cat theory" about earthquakes is held in high regard by many San Joseans, not the least among them being County Geologist Berkland. Reading the *Mercury News* lost-pets ads daily, he has perceived than an upsurge in strayed felines often presages a good shake, tending to reinforce his moon-sun-earth gravity calculations. Berkland also keeps close track of the spouting of the Calistoga geyser, having discerned frequent pre-earthquake irregularities in its interval. Combining his data from all these sources, he has formulated what he calls a "triple GG" parlay for quake forecasting: "gravity gradients," "geyser gap," and "gone *gatos*."

(Research at the University of California, incidentially, suggests that pet restlessness may have considerable validity as an earthquake harbinger, involving animals' ability to hear sound frequencies inaudible to humans.)

There remains in the Bay Area and elsewhere a diminishing "earthquake gentry"—the survivors of the Big One, the San Francisco calamity of "aught-six." Some of them are in my family, and early in life I

The new San Jose Post Office lost the top of its clock tower in the 1906 earthquake. Restored, the sandstone edifice became the Public Library in the 1930s and is now the Museum of Art.

learned that the proper term of reference is "earthquake and fire," never "earthquake" alone. The shake itself lasted, depending upon one's reference source, a mere 40 to 75 seconds, not counting aftershocks. The fire burned for four days.

In San Francisco 490 blocks were destroyed, mainly by the flames, and the damage was comparable from San Jose to Santa Rosa. The *World Almanac* puts the catastrophe's death toll at 452, a figure demonstrably low. It does not include at least 117 victims who perished in the rubble of Agnews State Hospital or 105 who died in Santa Rosa. It also probably excludes countless fatalities in San Francisco's Chinatown, where life was not held at a high premium by the authorities running the city.

Three-quarters of a century later the consequences of the disaster are still with us.

Why is the Bank of America the largest commercial bank in the world? Much of the reason has to do with the way it responded to the 1906 catastrophe, setting up shop on a wharf to start making reconstruction loans almost before the flames were out, though its liquid resources were only $80,000.

Why is the University of Santa Clara still situated in the city of that name? Because the earthquake and fire derailed a plan, then far advanced, to build a "Greater Santa Clara College" in open countryside west of Mountain View. Pledges of $250,000, counted on to start construction at the new site, suddenly dried up. (But the name the Jesuits gave their tract has clung to its crossroads through the decades: "Loyola Corners.")

On the 75th anniversary of the "San Francisco Horror," as a book published soon thereafter called it, I talked to as many survivors and their families as I could find. Everyone who lived through it, I learned, carried his own memories for life:

—Sen. Alan Cranston's grandmother, Jane MacGregor Cranston, wrote to the senator's parents, who were in Pasadena when the earthquake struck, "We saw strange things. A tall man walked along wearily, and when asked if he was ill or unfortunate, replied, 'I was worth $100,000 yesterday, but today my store is burned up, and I have just 40 cents in my pocket.'"

—Former San Josean Jane Blume, who was 11 years old in 1906, had arrived in San Francisco with her mother from Kansas City only two weeks before the earthquake. They had taken a housekeeping room on Mission Street, and as the street split open and houses all around them came crashing down, Jane's mother told her, "Pray, for the end of the world has come."

—For Marion Northup, a 10-year-old living in Santa Clara, the earthquake was, strangely, fun. Seventy-five years later she recalled, "I wasn't frightened a bit. We kids made a lark of it. Even now earthquakes don't bother me. They never have." In Santa Clara, she remembered, "The churches, everything built of brick, came down. The P.M. Mill went flat. My father worked there, and that ended his job; so we moved to Nevada."

—Anna Escobar of Fremont, a teenager in 1906, remembered standing on a fence in Mission San Jose and sighting the flames that were consuming San Francisco 30 miles northwest. Her half-sister, Angeline Martin, was living in San Francisco and was an eyewitness to the collapse of its $6 million City Hall: "The pillars just caved in, and the whole thing came down."

—Curt Bailey lived on East Santa Clara Street where San Jose Hospital stands now. Setting out on foot after the quake to reconnoiter, he found St. Patrick's Church at Ninth and Santa Clara in ruins, its tower collapsed across the streetcar tracks. San Jose High School at Seventh and San Fernando was likewise a rubble pile. Later the 12-year-old Curt got a job at 50 cents a day cleaning the mortar off the high school's bricks so that they could be reused.

San Jose Mercury News

St. Patrick's Church, at Ninth and Santa Clara Streets, as Curt Bailey found it on the morning of April 18, 1906. Two later churches have since occupied the property, the current one serving since 1981 as cathedral of the Catholic Diocese of San Jose.

—Ethel Bergen of San Jose remembered how the earthquake reunited her father, then a newcomer to San Francisco, with a long lost friend from his hometown, Boston. He and his friend's wife turned up in the same bread line.

The most vivid recollection of Jim Bailey of Saratoga was a looter's corpse dangling from a phone pole near Market and Van Ness in San Francisco, pursuant to Mayor Eugene Schmitz's no-nonsense proclamation of martial law:

> The federal troops, the members of the regular police force, and all special police officers have been authorized by me to kill any and all persons found engaged in looting or in the commission of any other crime.

In San Jose, the proclamation of Mayor G.D. Worswick was less drastic. He imposed a 7:30 P.M. curfew, barred citizens from the business district, and warned that lawlessness would be "repressed with a heavy hand."

Anna Bastian, who would later become the switchboard operator at Farmers Union Hardware in San Jose, was ending her last night as a resident of Santa Cruz when the big jolt came. Her family was to move that day to Sacramento, but by nightfall, after three false starts, they had only reached Watsonville in a stagecoach driven by a drunken coachman.

"First we boarded a narrow-gauge train for San Jose," Anna recalled, "and we got through the second tunnel but the third had caved in; so we turned back. Then they sent another train that was to go around through Watsonville, but close to Aptos the track had sunk."

Next, Anna's grandfather chartered a stage which started over the mountains, but slides blocked the road; so once again the family turned back, this time to Soquel.

"While the driver stopped in Soquel to water the horses," Anna related, "he somehow got a bottle of whiskey. By the time we got near Watsonville he didn't know much about what he was doing. Late in the afternoon he drove us into a ditch. A traveling salesman took the reins and drove us the rest of the way."

Anna's party, the first that had gotten through to Watsonville from the coast that day, was able to dispel a rampant rumor that a tidal wave had washed Santa Cruz off the map. That night Anna slept on a couch in the lobby of the Mansion House, a Watsonville hotel. Next morning the party forded the Pajaro River and went on to Morgan Hill, where a railroad agent flagged down a San Jose-bound train. The San Jose depot was packed with refugees from San Francisco. One vignette would remain forever in Anna's

San Jose Mercury News
In a good shake, a bottle shop is not the best place to be. The late Bill Young surveys wreckage in Pala Shopping Center liquor store after a quake on September 4, 1955.

memory: "A woman wandering aimlessly in a negligee and slippers—and a beautiful fur coat. She was carrying a cage with a polly parrot; that's all she had."

Few stories told me by the San Francisco earthquake survivors matched the tale of mystery, terror, violence, and skulduggery I heard from Florence Schroder of Saratoga, who was 1 year old in 1906:

"Exactly where I was born I have never been quite sure. I was dug out of the debris. My natural parents were in San Francisco; where I was is controversial. I get one story from my brother and another from my cousins, and according to the testimony in my custody trial I was in a nursing home for infants. My mother was ill.

"I must have been dropped in the fire, because I had nightmares about it until I was 13 or 14 years old. I always dreamed of being in a room circled by fire, and I was in one of those old-fashioned white iron cribs, and in my nightmare it would roll across the room. Just about the time it got ready to roll into the fire, it would roll back in the other direction to another wall of flame. I guess the building went down, because I would have the feeling of falling into complete blackness.

"It was a couple of days, as I understand it, before they found me. They dug me out, thinking I was dead. My skull was badly fractured, and I carry the scars to prove it; I have an indentation you can almost put a quarter into. And on my left hand, part of my index finger is gone."

Florence went through a series of foster homes, good and bad. One couple whipped her often, and she was taken from them when her crying was overheard. She ended up with a well-to-do family named Thurston, whose name she took. The Thurstons ran a cigar and candy store, with a branch post office, at 23rd and Folsom Streets. Florence's greatest trauma came when she was six years old:

"Mr. and Mrs. Thurston brought me in one day, and this strange woman, Mrs. Cordy, was there. They said they had to tell me something, that they were not my real parents, that this woman was my mother. I was terrified. I wouldn't go near her. It wasn't long before some shyster lawyer got wind of the story and started this very notorious custody trial, and it was in all the papers. My real mother didn't want me, but this lawyer was looking for a judgeship. I remember his saying he didn't care if he took this child from the lap of luxury and put her in the direst poverty, as long as he put her back with her mother."

In the end the Thurstons got to keep Florence, giving her a fine education in classical music. Later, grown up, she looked up her natural mother—the "Mrs. Cordy" who had frightened her so—and two brothers. But from them she never got good answers to the mysteries of her life.

Many who lived through the 1906 disaster deemed it an act of divine retribution. But the Rev. J.V. Combs, pastor of the destroyed First Christian Church in San Jose, rejected this idea in an article published not long afterward in the *Christian Standard*. He wrote:

> Many foolish things have been said. I attended an open-air meeting (where) almost all spoke of this earthquake as being a visitation of Providence. Some declared God sent it to punish for our wickedness... I am not in accord with this folly. The quake would have been just as severe if every man on the coast had been a saint; it would not have been more severe if all had been sinners. It would have occurred just as it did if there had not been one human being west of the mountains.

The same theme echoed through a bit of doggerel someone penned in San Francisco, where in the wake of the catastrophe Hotaling's Distillery remained intact on Montgomery Street:

> *If it be true God spanked the town*
> *For being much too frisky,*
> *Why did He burn the churches down*
> *And save Hotaling's whiskey?*

CHAPTER XVI
The Decoy Hooker

On the tree-shaded southern fringe of "downtown," families once lived serenely in stately Victorians. Then the street girls, the pimps, the junkies, and the muggers moved in.

It is almost time for Sharon Young's shift to start, and she is choosing her working outfit for the day. She ponders which wig to wear—the Farrah Fawcett job, the Afro, or one of the fluffy things.

The rest of her costume will be about what the typical housewife would choose for shopping—slacks and a blouse, attractive but not provocative. And she will probably wear a coat of some sort, to hide her microphone and gun. She will also select a bulky purse, one big enough to hold a tape recorder.

Thus fitted out, Sharon will proceed to her work station, a sidewalk near Second and Reed Streets, where she will stroll a little, smiling now and then. If she does her job well, she will be propositioned, perhaps a dozen times in her eight-hour shift. To the men on the street, afoot or slowly circling in cars, she will appear as anything but what she is, a cop of 15 years' standing on the San Jose force who on other days (and nights) drives a patrol car in uniform.

Sharon is a symbol of downtown San Jose in transition. She grew up there in the 1950s, attending Horace Mann and Jefferson Elementary Schools. So she remembers how it used to be. Even by then, South Second Street might have passed its prime as a residential neighborhood, but the families still living there enjoyed their stately if aging Victorians and their proximity to the bustle of the shopping district two or three blocks to the north.

Time has changed all that.

First the shopping malls on the outskirts dried up the fashionable downtown retail trade, and the city's heart became a forlorn wasteland of empty storefronts, flea-bag hotels, off-beat enterprises ranging from tattoo parlors to massage parlors, a few stubborn old-line businesses struggling for survival, and acres of vacant lots awaiting promised urban renewal. Then Interstate 280 sliced across the scene, ripping out scores of genteel old homes and inundating the rest in its smog and its roar. Several old churches abandoned the neighborhood, following their congregations to the outlying bedroom districts, where they put up magnificent new edifices.

Into the void thus created came the porno flicks, the adult bookstores, the streetwalkers with their pimps, the drug pushers and junkies, molesters, fast-buck artists, and muggers. San Jose gained one of the authentic badges of metropolitanism: a visible underworld. For the police, containment of this urban chancre has become a never-ending battle in which Sharon Young is an inestimable resource.

She never imagined her role in the battle when in 1966, answering a classified ad, she took a civil service examination and became an identification officer on the San Jose police force. Women were second class citizens in the department then, used mainly to strip-search women prisoners, baby-sit juveniles, and ride along when women had to go to jail. But after the department had its own women's-rights uprising, in the form of a protracted court skirmish, Sharon became one of the first 14 women to gain full patrol officer status.

She is an old hand now. She has patrolled every beat from the downtown core to East San Jose and Blossom Valley, so proficiently that rookies green from the Police Academy are assigned to ride with her to learn the ropes. But when she is on decoy duty, her job becomes a game.

"It's a dangerous game," she says, "but just a game. You're acting a role, and sometimes you wonder how convincing you are. It's fun when they really believe you're who you're portraying, when they really think you're a prostitute. The reason I'm in this job is, I love the excitement."

The john who approaches Sharon on the street will be sorry. She will lead him to a room in a hooker district motel, unlock the door, and let him enter first. Inside, a male officer will flash a badge and tell him, "You're under arrest for solicitation for prostitution."

The words turn men's blood to ice water.

"What happens is," Sharon has found, "their whole lives flash before them. They think their wives and their employers or employees are all going to know. We thought a couple of them were going to have heart attacks."

Thus cornered, johns sometimes turn violent.

"One fellow we had to fight off was a contractor from up the Peninsula. It took three of us to control him," Sharon recalls. "A lot of them are really scared because they don't know for sure we're the police, that we aren't somebody who's going to rip them off. 'Cause that happens. It's surprising how many of these men are carrying a lot of money. One had his company payroll on him; it was a Friday afternoon, and he had about $3,500 in cash. People would kill you for a lot less."

Sharon's "clientele" reflects the times. Not all of her cruising johns are the dregs of the town. A lot of them are family men, Silicon Valley executives taking the afternoon off. The premise of the decoy game, Sharon says, is, "If we can discourage the johns, the girls will go somewhere else."

She likes some of the girls, who flock to San Jose from places like Sacramento (where it's "too tough") or Oakland (where the johns are "too cheap"). When one of them, a 20-year-old regular, was picked up, she had john-inflicted cigarette burns on her breasts and bullet wounds on her arm. Another had stab wounds in her back and a bullet hole in her chest, the latter inflicted by her pimp. She had been raped twice within a month.

"Why do you keep coming back?" Sharon asked.

"The money. It's good down here."

That told Sharon a lot. The going rate was $20 a trick. It was mid-afternoon, and the woman had $160 on her. The john who had stabbed her, she said, was "a business type."

"And you know," says Sharon, "she wasn't a bad gal. You'd talk to her and she was kind of a sweet person."

If the hooker district were only a mart for sex, the police might ignore it, but it is also a breeder of violence from mayhem to murder. The johns are often armed, and Sharon knows there is ominous potential for homicide in every contact she makes.

"One time I was down on Reed Street," she recounts, "and this kid had been watching me, this kid about 14. Finally he walked up to me and made a pretty crude remark. He said he'd pay me $20. So I said OK, and after he was arrested we found no money on him. The only thing in his possession was a large knife. My impression was that he intended to rape and rob me. I'm sure he had raped or robbed other prostitutes down there, but they weren't about to report it. This guy had been around—for 14 years old."

Another woman officer on decoy duty was solicited by a pimp who demanded her purse on the spot. "Either you give me your money and start working for me," he said, "or I'll have someone take a pipe to you." Back-up officers moved in fast.

The typical streetwalker is lonely and defenseless. Not Sharon when she plays the role. She is not only armed, bugged, and wired for sound, but she has four back-up men on her team, two of whom keep her constantly in view. When the vice detail makes a big sweep in the hooker district, putting five women on the streets at once, it means 25 officers are tied up for the shift. The policewomen make a game of their job at times like that, competing to see who can attract the most johns.

In her play-acting, like any actress, Sharon must stick closely to a script. In talking with a john, she must give wide berth to anything approaching entrapment. For an arrest, two elements are essential in the conversation: mention of a sex act and an offer to pay. Both must be introduced by the prospective customer; when the case goes to court, the tapes must confirm that Sharon did not put ideas in his mind that weren't already there.

"Are you dating?" is the client's usual opener. Sharon can say "yes" without jeopardizing her case, but she must wait for him to say, "How much?" Then she answers with her own question, "How much do you pay?" If the john mentions a figure, he is hooked.

Sharon says there are odd variations. Sometimes a john asks point-blank, "Are you a cop?" Her standard parry, "No, are you?" always seem to satisfy.

"The johns play a lot of word games," she says. "If you've done enough decoy work, you know what they are."

Sex for sale will never end, but Police Chief Joe McNamara sees the hooker district and the violence it generates fading away as urban renewal gives San Jose a heart transplant.

In the meantime he will go on using decoys, not only in whore roles but in victim roles as well. Cops like Sharon regularly undertake rape and robbery decoy assignments, setting themselves up to be attacked, mugged, or ripped off.

It can be chilling work. On rape decoy duty once, Sharon was strolling down East Santa Clara Street when one of her cover officers came by and whispered, "Just keep walking. You're being followed by a rapist who garrotes his victims." Experiences like that have left her with mixed emotions.

"You really want to accomplish your goal, which is to get these people off the street," she says. "But you half-heartedly hope that nothing happens, too."

Sharon, now in her early 40s but younger looking, knows that time will overtake her as a decoy hooker, just as it overtakes the movie queen, the pro ball player, or the real hooker. But not necessarily soon. As a robbery decoy once, she made herself up as a real hag. She was supposed to be an aging wino.

"I went down to detox and picked up some old clothes," she relates, "a coat with the lining hanging out, nylons with holes, the world's ugliest dress, a wig, blue glasses. I felt like an idiot, which was the impression I wanted to give."

In that get-up Sharon feigned a boozy stupor and walked around downtown with bills sticking out of her purse to tempt muggers. That was one time she failed.

"Not one robber came near," she says, "...but I still got solicited for prostitution."

San Jose Mercury News

The Akron *over San Jose, May 1932. At right, the First National Bank Building at First and Santa Clara Streets (now the remodeled Bank of the West).*

CHAPTER XVII
The Temples Of High-Tech

The would-be D.A. boasted, "I'm the only candidate who knows the difference between a computer chip and a potato chip."

Napoleon J. Menard, the blunt, pugnacious district attorney of a quarter-century ago, would have been bewildered by the rhetoric of the 1982 campaign for his old job.

Candidate Julius Finkelstein listed prominently, among his prosecutorial qualifications, a master's degree in computer science. He proclaimed, "I'm the only candidate who knows the difference between a computer chip and a potato chip."

The boast was not so irrelevant as it would have seemed to Menard—if indeed it had not sounded to him like gibberish. In the years he had been in his grave, his old Santa Clara County domain had filled up not just with ticky-tacky tract homes and row house condominiums, but also with endless acres of low, sleek industrial buildings dedicated to the pursuit and exploitation of high technology. They hugged the landscape from the Stanford hills to Coyote Valley. And on the heels of the scientists, engineers, technicians, and overnight entrepreneurs had come the fast-buck artists, black marketeers, gray marketeers, thieves, and spies. Within the offices, blueprint rooms, laboratories, and component storage areas, a fifth column of corrupt employees was stealing secrets and circuits. A new breed of burglar was specializing in computer terminals. There were prosecutions for industrial espionage and international espionage. The valley had become, in

the phrase of *Mercury News* investigators Pete Carey and Steve Johnson, an electronics "Casbah."

The bad, of course, was only the flip side of the success story. The semiconductor, the transistor, and the integrated circuit had poured fabulous wealth into the county, creating a new economic and intellectual gentry and giving this corner of the world instant recognition from Tokyo to Singapore to Moscow.

How had it all happened? How had Santa Clara County become to electronics what Detroit is to automobiles and Hartford is to insurance? Whence had come Silicon Valley?

It had started long before one might suspect.

Before the transistor, there was the "tube." Now a whole generation has grown up in a solid-state world, scarcely seeing one, but in the fondly recalled "great age of radio," the vacuum tube was as much a part of the scene as the electric light bulb, which it resembled.

Behind the polished veneer of every parlor console was an array of the silvered, teardrop-shaped bulbs. The tube was a status symbol; the more tubes, the more powerful (and expensive) the set. The family with a 10-tube radio was probably the richest on the block.

When a tube set was turned on, it had to "warm up." Not until the current had been flowing for a few

The Macon entering its Moffett Field hangar, 1934.

U.S. Naval Air Station, Moffett Field

seconds would the tubes start to glow softly, signaling that a stream of electrons was passing between the elements inside. Only then would the music begin.

The "radio tube," as everyone called it, was more formally the Audion, invented in 1906 by Dr. Lee De Forest, a young man caught up in the early romance of "wireless." At first he did not fully discern the usefulness of his own invention. It was a "valve" that controlled the flow of electrons through a vacuum, but to what end?

Not until 1912 did De Forest, working in a little house at 913 Emerson Street, Palo Alto, put his Audion through the historic series of tests which would establish its world-shaking capabilities. He had developed it originally as a detector—a better device for snatching from the ether the puny dit-dah signals of the spark-gap wireless transmitters of the time. What he discovered in Palo Alto was two new uses for his tube: By hooking a series of Audions together, he found that a current—hence a radio signal or a distant telephone voice—could be amplified infinitely; so the stage was set for the loudspeaker to replace the earphone. De Forest also found that if he recycled an electron stream through the same tube twice, the current would *oscillate* in a feedback effect. In a loudspeaker hooked up to his tube, the oscillations produced only a high-pitched whistle, but when fed into the antenna of a transmitter, they became the high-frequency waves needed to broadcast the human voice.

Thus the work De Forest did in Palo Alto made the transcontinental telephone possible and gave birth to the commercial radio industry.

De Forest died in 1961 at the age of 87, having made and lost several fortunes; he left only $1,250 in cash. But he had lived to hear himself hailed as "the father of radio," and five years before his death, the Emerson Street house had been declared a historic landmark. A sign erected by the Palo Alto Historical Association identified it as the "Birthplace of Electronics."

A sad denouement was on the way, however. By 1978 the house had a new owner, no history buff, who armed himself with a city permit and bulldozed it. The Historical Association was furious when it heard about the demolition a month after the fact. But by then, the "first site" of Silicon Valley was a vacant lot.

It is hard to discern any cause-and-effect linkage between De Forest's 1912 research in Palo Alto and the emergence of a fabulous electronics community on the same ground, give or take a few miles, 70 years later. The only connection would seem to be an accident of geographic propinquity. If any single dominant force in the emergence can be identified, it is probably Stanford University. Ever since Herbert Hoover graduated

in 1895, the Farm at Palo Alto has been nurturing engineers, scientists, and priests for the temples of high-tech. Yet it was not Stanford that drew De Forest to Palo Alto; he came there to work for the old Federal Telegraph Company, whose wires ran up and down the Pacific Coast. The role of Fate seems to have exceeded that of the university.

Indeed, Silicon Valley appears to have come into being through the working of a mystic force as elusive but as inexorable as the electron itself. The fluke, the lucky break, the unforeseen consequence, the ironic turn of events, and the happy accident of timing recur again and again throughout the story. One can almost perceive a "Dalai Lama" reincarnation phenomenon in the fact that the year 1913, which saw De Forest leave Palo Alto for fields afar, also saw William Shockley arrive there at age 3. Thirty-six years later Shockley would inherit De Forest's mantle by co-inventing the transistor, which would render the Audion tube almost obsolete.

Turning points in the silicon saga were often undiscernable when they came. When Congress voted in 1931 to accept the community's gift of a thousand acres of the Posolmi Rancho in the South Bay lowlands for a Navy air base, the admirals were not thinking in terms electronic.* Nor were they dreaming of space flight, which was still Buck Rogers stuff. They were beckoned by the equally exciting technological frontier of lighter-than-air flight. So at Moffett Field they built the largest hangar in the world, 1,133 feet long and 308 feet wide, to house the largest dirigible in the world, the *U.S.S. Macon*. The silver airship was 785 feet long and 133 feet wide—dimensions not too different from those of today's Transamerica Pyramid.

For three years people in the Santa Clara Valley, including the author, marveled as this cigar-shaped miracle and its sister ship, the *Akron*, cruised majestically through their skies. To me as a child, the sight of these ships hovering above San Jose was the most awesome in my experience. If they were to return today, I am sure it would still be. It was like watching the *Queen Mary* and *Queen Elizabeth* gliding overhead at low altitude.

Double tragedies would write a premature finale to the era of the big airships. First the *Akron* plummeted into the turbulent Atlantic in a blinding electrical storm off New Jersey on April 4, 1933, with loss

---

*In 1929 when the future Moffett Field was in the talking stage, one *Mercury Herald* headline called it the "Posolmi Air Base." By 1931 when President Hoover signed the bill to create it, it was the Sunnyvale Air Base. It was renamed Moffett Field in May, 1933, the month after Rear Admiral William A. Moffett, a lighter-than-air pioneer, was killed in the crash of the *Akron*.

U.S. Naval Air Station, Moffett Field

Inside the Macon's hangar, it was roomy enough for numerous small, non-rigid airships akin to today's Goodyear blimps to be tucked in around the edges. The nose of one of them (arrow) is visible in shadows, lower right.

of 73 crewmen.* Then, on February 12, 1935, the *Macon* found its own watery grave of Point Sur. Though all but two members of the 81-man *Macon*

crew were saved, the Navy's greatest lighter-than-air adventure was over.

Suddenly the huge silver hangar at Moffett was the most visible white elephant in the world, and the field itself had become an embarrassment.

But again a reincarnation came into play. In 1939 the National Advisory Committee on Aeronautics chose Moffett from among 54 sites throughout the country as a base for its assaults on two new and even more challenging frontiers—supersonic travel and outer space. The NACA erected the world's largest wind tunnel, rivaling in size the *Macon*'s cavernous, forlornly deserted home nearby. The tunnel became the centerpiece of Ames Aeronautical Laboratory

*Less than 11 months earlier, on May 9, 1932, the *Mercury Herald* had run a confident if naive headline, "*Akron* Model of Safety Able to Ride Any Storm." The story called the ship "one of the safest flying devices which ever left the ground" and detailed its supposed invulnerability to rain, snow, hail, cold, heat, wind, and ironically lightning: "The metal framework of the rigid airship forms a 'Faraday cage' where lightning, if it hits the airship, is distributed and escapes harmlessly through the engine exhaust."

The Akron *prepares to moor near the skeleton of Sunnyvale's big hangar, May, 1932.*   San Jose Mercury News

(named for Joseph S. Ames, who had been NACA chairman). And it was only natural that in 1955, when Lockheed needed to relocate its Missiles Systems Division, with its own wind tunnel, it would move in right next door. Stanford was important in Lockheed's decision, too; the company leased 22 acres from the university for its laboratory.

Lockheed has been on the cutting edge of missile technology ever since, from the time of the Polaris and Trident projects. It is part of the space race, controlling Air Force surveillance satellites and making the heat-retardant tiles for the Space Shuttle.

When Jack McCullough began tinkering with radio, making his own crystal set when he was in the sixth grade in the early 1920s, his father told him he was wasting his time.

"There's no money in it," the father said.

But by the time Jack was 14 he had his ham operator's license, and in 1933, in a classic success scenario still replaying, he teamed up with another ham, a 1926 graduate of Los Gatos High named Bill Eitel, to manufacture De Forest's vacuum tubes. Founded with borrowed money, the Eitel-McCullough firm (trade name Eimac) remained a modest venture through the 1930s. By the end of the decade it had only 17 employees in its plant on the Peninsula.

Then it was overtaken by the march of history. War clouds gathered, and Eimac found itself the sole supplier of radar transmitting tubes for the Western Alliance. Overnight its work force grew to 3,000.

Radar, then so new that even its name was top secret, depended on the klystron tube, the invention of a couple of other tinkerers, Russell and Sigurd Varian of Palo Alto. Russell Varian had been thought dull in grade school; reading, writing, and spelling eluded him, and he flunked so often that he started high school four years late with a full-blown inferiority complex. But his problem was only that he thought in unconventional ways. The "slow thinker" struggled through to a master's degree at Stanford and later founded Varian Associates.

Ultimately, Eitel-McCullough was merged into the Varian empire, though the Eimac brand name lives on.

David Packard, a tall, muscular football player, and stocky, red-haired William Hewlett graduated from Stanford together in 1934, an inauspicious time. The blight of the Great Depression was on the land. Hollywood, which by chance would give Hewlett and Packard a big boost at the right time later, would scarcely have cast them as titans-to-be.

They went their separate ways for five years but then, with an investment of $538, they joined to start manufacturing electronic devices in the one-car garage of Packard's rented home at 367 Addison Street, Palo Alto. Their early products included a weight reducing machine, an electronic harmonica tuner, a foul line indicator for bowling alleys, and a diathermy machine for the Palo Alto Medical Clinic.

Then, at a trade show in Portland, they exhibited an audio-oscillator that Hewlett had invented. It drew the interest of people from Walt Disney Studios, preparing to produce the landmark movie *Fantasia*, featuring wrap-around sound so innovative that only a few theaters could show the picture properly. Disney bought eight of the oscillators, and Hewlett-Packard was on its way.

During World War II, H-P snowballed from 20 employees to 175, manufacturing measuring devices. By 1954 its sales were $12 million a year; by 1982 they were $1.2 billion for the first quarter.

In 1980 the *World Almanac* listed both Hewlett and Packard among the 22 richest Americans, both in the $400-$600 million bracket. They had not quite overtaken the du Ponts, Mellons, Gettys, Rockefellers, and Hunts, but they were far out in front of the Kennedys.

The same sort of process that gave us Eimac, Varian Associates, and Hewlett-Packard has never stopped working:

—In 1942 another ham radio operator, Jo Emmett Jennings, who had worked his way through San Jose State building radios and loudspeakers, went into partnership with Calvin Townsend and Arthur Neild to make condensers for the Signal Corps. Their business flourished when Jennings discovered (to the delight of a worried Army) that nickel could be substituted in the condensers for the war-scarce metal tantalum. Their 20 by 30-foot quarters gave way to a sprawling plant in an orchard, at what the wartime *Mercury Herald* called an "obscure spot," McLaughlin Avenue and Story Road. By the time the founders sold out in 1961 to the International Telephone and Telegraph Co., creating today's ITT Jennings, 450 persons worked there. The plant is still in use, but no way obscure anymore; Interstate 280 traffic roars past outside.

—In 1970 Dr. Gene M. Amdahl quit his 18-year job as a computer designer for IBM and announced he was forming his own company to compete. It was a bold gamble; IBM had outdistanced such giants as General Electric, RCA, and Xerox in the computer field. Five years and $50 million of debt later, Amdahl Corporation rolled its first mainframe computer out the door, and by 1978 it had 10 per cent of the market. The struggle for financing had taken its toll, however. A Japanese firm owned 36 per cent of Amdahl's stock; a Chicago company owned 35 per cent. The founder's equity in the company bearing his name stood at only 2 per cent. His boldness surfaced anew and he resigned as a chairman and director. Then he started the cycle all over again by founding still another computer firm, Acsys Corporation.

—Electrical engineer Nolan Bushnell was not yet 30 when in 1972 he conceived the prototype video game, Pong, and with $500 founded Atari, the Sunnyvale firm that would produce it. Seven years later he was living in a big house and driving a Rolls Royce; Pong was being played in 13 million American homes; and Atari had been sold to Warner Communications for $28 million. The restless Bushnell had turned to another project that by 1982 was equally successful, Pizza Time Theatre. Starting with one San Jose store in 1977, it had acquired 112 outlets in the United States, Canada, and Australia and had annual sales of $32.6 million.

When in 1943 International Business Machines took over the old Temple Laundry building at 16th and St. John Streets to make cards for its accounting

machines, the San Jose Chamber of Commerce was delighted. It had already launched a drive for postwar industry. Nothing in the modest notices of the new facility, however, signalled that the seed had been planted for a wholly new lifestyle and economy in Santa Clara Valley.

The first electronic digital computer in the world was still four years in the future. Called ENIAC (Electronic Numerical Integrator and Computer), it would be built in 1947 at the University of Pennsylvania—a monster filling a gymnasium-sized room, with 18,800 vacuum tubes that would keep burning out; when they all heated up at once, they would turn the room into an oven.

The builders of ENIAC had no way of knowing that even as they worked, William Shockley and two of his colleagues at Bell Laboratories were nearing completion of an eight-year project that would shortly make their machine an oversized antique.

Shockley's experimentation would produce in December, 1947, a device the size of a pencil eraser, a "sandwich" of some such semiconductor material as

San Jose Mercury News

Dictator Khrushchev visits the San Jose IBM plant with Andrei Gromyko (hat). At far left, IBM President Thomas Watson Jr.

silicon or germanium, which would do the same job as a vacuum tube without ever heating up or burning out. The world would soon come to know the device as a "transistor."

Several more years would pass before anyone, save perhaps the wildest theoretician, would contemplate reducing not only the transistor but all the circuitry that went with it to a quarter-inch silicon chip. That big breakthrough would come in 1957, giving birth to Fairchild Semiconductor.

Meanwhile the technological seed planted in IBM's old St. John Street laundry had taken root in fertile soil; the San Jose growing conditions proved ideal. In 1952 IBM added a laboratory in a rented building at 99 Notre Dame Avenue. It was just out the back door of our old *Mercury News* shop downtown, but in the newsroom we had no conception of the monumental work going on there—design that would lead in the long run to IBM's landmark RAMAC (Random Access) computer.

What little we wrote about our back-fence neighbor discloses when read now that to us, the electronics vocabulary was an alien tongue. We were not conversant, or at least not comfortable, with the word "computer" yet. Quaintly the *News* reported in 1953 that the IBM people were working with "high-speed printing and arithmetic." When the RAMAC was finally unveiled, our headline called it a "calculating jukebox."

It was in 1955 that IBM announced its purchase of 190 rural acres at Monterey Highway and Cottle Road for a plant that would, at the outset, produce the RAMAC. By 1959 this complex became the computer showplace of the world. Nikita Khrushchev, touring the United States that year in the first great thaw of the Cold War, visited it with Andrei Gromyko and Henry Cabot Lodge, carrying his tray through the cafeteria line for a chicken lunch.

Judging from the way *USSR* magazine reported the visit later, the cafeteria impressed the dictator more than the production line. "We should follow your example and build more self-service lunchrooms," Khruschchev told IBM President Thomas Watson Jr. He said nothing about the RAMAC.

After a 1972 brainstorming session with a Stanford researcher about the potential of the silicon chip, reporter Dale Mead sat down at his *Mercury News* typewriter to write a story that sounded (as it was supposed to) like science fiction:

> Imagine a small all-electric watch without hands—only a face that displays the time in numerals....
>
> Or imagine a supercalculator small enough to put in your shirt pocket which figures calculations like square roots and logarithms silently and instantaneously.
>
> Then visualize a picture-frame television that you can hang on your wall or a small, computerized home learning machine....
>
> Applied to automobiles, the microcircuits could be used to control your carburetor and ignition more accurately and compute how many more miles you can go on the gas you've got left.

It is hard to realize now how other-worldly Mead's words sounded when he wrote them—for in 10 years they have all come true.

Don Hoeffler of *Microelectronics* magazine takes credit for coining the name "Silicon Valley," though its origin is in dispute. Wherever the name started, it fulfills a prediction that Calvin Townsend of the Jennings firm gave *Mercury Herald* reporter Hal Martin in 1945. With World War II ending, Townsend looked forward to the role his company might assume in peacetime. Postwar orders, he thought, would surpass the wartime business from the Signal Corps.

"As a matter of fact," he went on, "we are optimistic enough to believe that the San Jose area will become the center of the electronics industry on the West Coast."

He might have said "in the world."

Index

Acsys Corporation, 107
Adams Street, 6
Ager, Susan, x
Agnew, 66
Agnews State Hospital, 93
Akron, airship, 100, 103, 105
Albee, Wilson "Bill," 3, 44
Allard, Bernard J., 45
Allen, Bruce F., 15, 45
Allen, Helen Kamp, ix
Alma, 5
Almaden, 5
Almaden Avenue, 1, 3, 35
Alquist, Alfred E., 49, 91
Alum Rock Park, ix, 5
Alviso, 42
Amdahl, Gene M., 106
Amdahl Corporation, 106
American Civil Liberties Union, 54n, 56
American Institute of Architects, 66
American Savings Building, 27
Ames, Joseph S., 106
Ames Aeronautical Laboratory, 31, 105
Amin, Idi, 17
Andrews Sisters, 25
Apple computers, 76
Appleton, Larry, 6
Aptos, 95
Arbuckle, Clyde, 4
Army, U.S., 87, 88-89
    Signal Corps, 106, 108

Army Reserve armory, 68
Atari, Inc., 107
Atherton, 79
Auzerais House, 27

Baez, Joan, 25
Bailey, Curt, 94
Bailey, Jim, 95
Baltimore *Sun*, 92
Bank of America, 2, 60, 65, 93
Bank of Italy, 2, 60, 65
Bank of the West, 35, 37, 58, 69, 100
Bardeen, John, 19
Barrett, Dick, 17, 39
Barrie, Christie, 42
Bastian, Anna, 95
Bayard, Sheldon ("Abil Layman"), 23-24, 64
Bee, Carlos, 83
Befame, Jeannette, 41
Bell Telephone Laboratories, 19, 107
Bellarmine College Preparatory, 3
Benedetti, Joan, 90
Bergen, Ethel, 95
Bergna, Louis, 56
Berkland, James, 92
Berlin, Germany, 69
Bernhardt, Clarisa, 92
Bigley, Charles, 7-9
Bigley, Mary, 8
Bigley Ambulance Co., 7
Bird, Rose, 17, 45-46

Bird Avenue, 6
Bissell, Dwight M., 38
Blackmore, Ray, 8
Black Panthers, 81-84
Blossom Valley, 98
Blume, Jane, 94
B'nai B'rith, 53
Bonaparte, Napoleon, 69
Bonelli, William, 15
Bradley, Clark, 7
Brattain, Walter H., 19
"Brick Hill", 1, 5
Broun, Heywood, 39
Brown, Bob, 6
Brown, Edmund G. "Jerry" Jr., 10, 11, 20, 45, 47, 84
Brown, Edmund G. "Pat" Sr., 10, 11, 12, 13, 20, 35, 47, 50, 77-78
Brown, Willie, 84
Brown Act, 9
Browning, James Jr., 45
Brzezinski, Zbigniew, 84
Buchanan, James, 27
Buck Shaw Stadium, 31
Burbank District, ix
Burkett, Sid, 90
Burnett, John, 73
Burnett, Peter, 73
Bushnell, Nolan, 107
Butcher's Corners, 4

Calaveras Fault, 91
California Committee for Better Legislation, 49, 50, 51
California Public Market, 36
California Trucking Association, 46
Calistoga geyser, 92
Callaghan, Raymond, 56
Call of the Wild, The, 3
Calloway, Hank, 2
Campbell (city), 27
Campbell, O.W. "Hump," 41
Canoas Creek, 1
Caputo, Dan, 7
Carey, Pete, 101
Carmichael, Hoagy, 41
Carmichael, Stokely, 41
Carter, Jimmy, 18, 77, 84
Casa Verde restaurant, 44
Century Plaza Hotel, 12
Chatton, Milton, 17-18
Christensen, Terry, 7
Christian Standard, 96
Christopher, George, 45, 77-78
Churchill, Winston, 79
City Hall, old, 2, 7-9, 38, 59, 64-67, 68
City Plaza, 2, 7, 65, 66
Civic Auditorium, 2, 30, 31, 59
Civic Center, 3, 4, 30, 67-70, 91
Civil War, 27
Clay Street, 6
Cleary, Don, 16

Cleaver, Eldridge, x, 81-86
Clifford, Clark, 28
Coalinga, 91
Coast and Geodetic Survey, 37
Coe, Charles W., 28
Coleman, Hugh C., 4
Coleman Avenue, 4
Colla, Joe, 45
College of the Pacific, 3
College Park, 1, 3
College Station, 5
Collier, Randolph, 5
Columbus, Christopher, 6
Columbus Park, 6
Combs, J.V., 96
Condon, Ralph, 56
Conn, Kenneth S., 40, 72-73, 75
Connolly, Matt, 28
Conroy, Paul E., 74-75
Cordy, Mrs., 96
County Administration Building, 59, 68
County Animal Control, 46
County Hospital (Valley Medical Center), 17
County Water Commission, 73
Courthouses, 60-64, 66, 68
Cow Palace, 16
Cox, Fred Parr, 47
Coyote Valley, 101
Cranston, Alan, 13, 28, 44, 80, 94
Cranston, Jane MacGregor, 94
Crittenden Street, 6
Crummey family, 1
Cupertino, 46, 82

Daily Worker, 38
Danielson, Wayne, 35
Davidson, Charles, 7
Davies family, 1
Davis, George T., 55
Davis, John F., 91
Davis, Smith, 36
De Anza College, 82, 83, 84, 86
De Anza Hotel, 39, 75
Deaver, Mike, 33
De Forest, Lee, 103, 106
Della Maggiore, Sam, 21
Dellums, Ronald V., 84
Democratic County Central Committee, 45
Democratic State Central Committee, 50
Detroit News, 18
Dewey, Thomas E., 10-11, 29
DeWitt, John L., 87, 89-90
Diaz, Andy, 21-23
DiMaggio, Joe, 3
Diocese of San Jose, 94
Diridon, Rodney, 92
Dooley, Tevis, 69
Dumbarton Bridge, 91
du Pont family, 106
Dylan, Bob, 84

Earl Carroll's Vanities, 24
Earthquakes, 91-96
East San Jose, 6, 98
Edwards, Don, 30
Eel River, 47
Eichmann, Adolf, 82
Eimac, 106
Eisenhower, Dwight D., 10
Eitel, Bill, 106
Eitel-McCullough, Inc., 106
El Capitan Bar, 39
El Dorado Street, 1, 3
El Mirador Hotel, 51, 79
Engle, Clair, 13, 20
ENIAC computer, 107
Equal Rights Amendment, 22
Escobar, Anna, 94

Fairchild, Patricia, 66
Fairchild Semiconductor, 108
Fairmont Hotel, 28 30, 79
Fantasia, 106
Farmers Union Hardware, 95
Farrell, Betty, 8
Farrell, Harry, 25, 32
        at Black Panther invasion, 81-66
        as copy boy, 36-38
        and "Money, Power, and Politics" series, 48-52
        personal history, ix, x
        in "slaughterhouse war", 72-76
Fawcett, Farrah, 97
Federal Telegraph Company, 103
Finch, Robert H., 45
Finkelstein, Julius, 101
First Christian Church, 96
First National Bank, 58, 100
Fisher, Mrs. Herbert, 33
Flood, Dick, 75
FMC Corporation, 13
Folsom Prison, 82
Food Villa, 5
Foothill College, 84
Ford, Gerald R., 18, 32-33, 45
Fowle, Eleanor, 28
Fowler, Lenore, 64-65, 66, 67
Fowler, Robert G. "Bob," 64
Freeman, Frank, 35
Fremont, 90, 94
Fremont, John C., 27
Fresno County, 20
Friedenrich, David, 14
Frost, David, 32
Fullerton, Gail P., 71

Gallagher family, 2
Garden Alameda complex, 33
Gardiner, Gertrude, 27
Gardner, Erle Stanley, 55
Garrigus, Charles B. "Gus," 20, 21
Garza, Al, 22, 24

General Electric Company, 33, 106
        General Electric Theater, 33
George, John, 83
Getty family, 106
"Ghlue, Dagobert," 17, 24-25
Gilroy, 76
Golden Gate Bridge, 91
Goldwater Barry, 16, 20-21, 45
Gonzales, Nick, 46
Goodwin, Clarence, 8
Goodyear blimps, 104
Goosetown, 1, 4, 7
Graham, Jack, 3
Graham Avenue, 3
Graham Field, 1, 2-3
Grand Island, Neb., 74-75
Grant, Ulysses S., 27
Graves, Richard, 12
Gromyko, Andrei, 108
Guadalupe River, 1, 3, 68
Gubser, Charles S., 33
Guinness Book of World Records, 21

Haldeman, H.R. "Bob," 32
Hall of Justice, 63
Hall of Records, 62, 63
Hamann, A.P. "Dutch," 7, 8, 73, 75
Hamline Street, 3, 4
Harding, Warren G., 24
Harrison, Benjamin, 27
Hart, Brooke, 44
Hayakawa, S.I., 45, 88
Hayes, Elystus L. "Dit," 36, 39, 40
Hayes family, 36-39
Hayes, Harold, 36, 39, 40
Hayes, Janet Gray, x, 23, 91
Hayes, J.O., 28
Hayes, Rutherford B., 27
Hayward Fault, 91
Hearst, Patty, 45
Hearst newspapers, 50
Hedding, Elijah, 3
Hedding Street, 3
Hewlett, William R., 106
Hewlett-Packard Co., 106
Hickey, Ben, 27
Hillings, Pat, 16
Hinrichs, Scott, 66
Hirano, J.S., 88
Hirohito, 89
Hitler, Adolf, 69, 70, 90
Hitt, Ben, 23
Ho Chi Minh, 46
Hoeffler, Don, 108
Holiday Inn, 32
Holiday Magic cosmetics, 77, 79
Hollister, 44, 91, 92
Hollywood, 24, 106
Hollywood High School, 90
"Holocaust", 57

Hoover, Herbert, 5, 27-28, 29, 103
Hoover Junior High School, x
Horace Mann School, 97
Hornbuckle, Howard, 56
Hotaling's Distillery, 96
Houser, Bob, 12
Hruby, Dan, 34
Hughes, Howard, 50-51
Humphrey, Hubert H., 44
Hunt family, 106
Hunt's Cannery, ix
Hutton, Bobby, 82, 85
Hutton, E.F. & Company, 36
Hyatt House, 30
Hyde Park, 1, 4

Interlude bar, 33
IBM Corporation (International Business Machines), 18, 107, 108
ITT (International Telephone & Telegraph Corporation), 106
    ITT Jennings, 106
Iran hostage crisis, 87
Irvington, 90

James, William F., 56
Japanese relocation 87-90
Jefferson School, 97
Jennings, Jo Emmett, 106
John Birch Society, 16
Johnson, Lyndon B., 12-13, 20-21, 30, 31, 33
Johnson, Steve, 101
Jones Street, 6
Jordan, David Starr, 28
Joshua Hendy Iron Works, 28, 29

Kaiser, Lee, 79
Kaiser Aluminum, 28
Keating, Thomas, 44
Keeler, James, 4
Kefauver, Estes, 13-15
Kennedy, John F., x, 12, 20, 27, 29-30, 70
Kennedy, Robert F., 13, 46-47
Kennedy family, 13, 106
Khrushchev, Nikita, 107, 108
Kiwanis Club, 25
Knaefler, Diane, 90
Knight, Goodwin J. "Goodie," 10-12, 35, 55
Knoche, Herman, 67, 68
Knowland, William F., 35
Knox Block, 59
Kopp, Charli, 32
Kreps, Theodore, 27
KRVE, 92
Kuchel, Thomas H., 79-80

Ladd, Leroy, 5
Lake County, 80
Langley, Rolly, 37
Larocca, Dorothy, 6

"Layman, Abil" (Sheldon Bayard), 23-24, 64
Leahy, David, 47
Le Baron Hotel, 33
L'Enfant, Pierre Charles, 69-70
Lennon Sisters, 25
Lenzen, Jacob, 66
Lenzen, Theodore, 66
Lexington Dam, 5, 44
Lick Observatory, 4
Liden, Oscar, 75
Lincoln, Abraham, 27, 79, 89
Lindsay, Francis, 45
Lippmann, Walter, 87
Live Oak High School, 15
Lockheed Missiles & Space Company, Inc. (Lockheed Missiles Systems Division), 106
Lockwood Charles, 35
Locust Street, 4
Lodge, Henry Cabot, 108
London, Jack, 3
Lone Hill, 5
Long Beach, 50-52
Long Beach Independent, Press-Telegram, 12, 50
Long's Drugs, 4
Loomis (city), 45
Loomis, Patricia, 6, 39
Los Altos, x, 24-25, 42
Los Altos Hills, 42
Los Angeles Daily News, 41
Los Angeles Times, 72
Los Gatos, ix, 5, 14, 43, 92
Los Gatos High School, 106
Lou's Village, 33
Loyola Corners, 4, 94
Lynch, John, 68
Lyon, Charles, 15

McAlister, Alister, 44
McBride, James, 44
McCabe Hall, 30
McCarthy, Eugene, 46
McCauley, Jim, 50
McCloskey, Paul N. "Pete," 33
McCullough, Jack, 106
McEnery, John P., 28-29
McEnery, Tom, 28
McKibben, Winton, 82
McKinley, William, 26, 27
McLaughlin Avenue, 6
McLean, Cliff, 40
McLemore, Henry, 87
McNamara, Joseph, 99
McNamara, Robert, 80
Macon, airship, 102-105
Mafia, 46
Manny's Cellar, 24
Mansion House, 95
Mao Tse-tung, 41
Marin County, 46, 78
Martin, Angeline, 94

Martin, Hal, 108
Mathewson, Ray, 4
Mayfair District, 6
Mayfield, 5
Mead, Dale F., 108
Melbourne (Australia) *Herald*, 92
Mellon family, 106
Menard, Napoleon J. "Nap," 55-57, 101
Mensa, 18
Meridian Corners, 1, 4
Meridian Road, 4
Meyers, Charles, 46
Microelectronics magazine, 108
Milliken Corners, 4
Mission San Jose, 94
Moffett, William A., 103n
Moffett Field, x, 102, 103, 105
Monroe Street, 6
Monterey *Peninsula Herald*, 37
Montgomery Street, 6
Mooney, Tom, 55
Morgan Hill, 15, 73, 88, 95
Moscow, USSR, 101
Mosk, Stanley, 16
Mountain View, 93
Mt. Diablo, 4
Moynihan, Daniel Patrick, 40
Moynihan, John, 40
Municipal Court Building, 68
Murdock, Steve, 38
Murphy, George, 13, 31, 32

Naglee Avenue, 6
Naglee Park, 6
National Advisory Committee on Aeronautics (NACA),
    105-106
National Aeronautics and Space Administration (NASA),
    31
National Enquirer, 92
National Guard armory, 68
National Women's Political Caucus, 21-22
Navy, U.S., 102-105
Neild, Arthur, 106
Newspaper Guild, 38, 39, 40, 75
Newton, Huey, 82
New Yorker magazine, 43
New York *Times*, 32
Nimitz, Chester, 35
Nixon, Richard, 16, 31-32, 33, 50-51, 84
Nobel, Alfred, 18
Nobel Prize, 17-19
Nofziger, Lyn, 33
Northup, Marion, 94

Oak Hill Mausoleum, 9
Oakland *Tribune*, 37
O'Brien's restaurant, 32
O'Connor, Percy, 53-54
Omohundro, Baxter, 78
Orchard Street, 1, 3

Orchard Supply Hardware, 5
Osmond, Donny and Marie, 25

Pacheco Pass, 20
Pacific Manufacturing Co. (P.M. Mill), 94
Pacific Telephone, 5-6
Packard, David, 106
Pajaro River, 95
Pala Shopping Center, 95
"Palmdale Bubble," 92
Palo Alto, 5, 28, 43, 46, 103, 106
Palo Alto Historical Association, 103
Palo Alto Medical Clinic, 106
Park Center, 3
Parkinson, Gaylord, 79
Pasadena, 94
Patrick, Dack, 78
Patrick, William Penn, 77-80
Paul VI, Pope, 44
Payne family, 36
Pearl Harbor, 41, 87, 88, 90
Pebble Beach, 33
Penney's building, 59-60
People's World, 38
Pera family, 1
Permanente Metals Corporation, 28
Pershing, John J., 90
Pestarino, Angelo, 56
Phinney, Milt, x, 41
Pizza Time Theatre, 107
Pleasant Hill, 82
Point Sur, 105
Polaris missile, 106
Polhemus, C.B., 6
Polhemus Street, 6
Pong game, 107
Posolmi Rancho, 103
Post Office, 2, 26, 60, 62, 93
Priest, Ivy Baker, 46
Priest Street, 6
Public Works Administration (PWA), 3, 59
Punch Bowl National Cemetery, 88

Queen Elizabeth, 103
Queen Mary, 103

Rafferty, Max, 80
RAMAC computer, 108
Ramparts magazine, 82, 83
RCA Corporation, 106
Reagan, Ronald, x, 10, 15, 16, 31, 33, 35, 77-78, 82, 84
Redwood City, 46
Reed, Sally, 91
Regan, Maude, 8
Reid-Hillview Airport, 64
Republican State Central Committee, 78
Republican County Central Committee, 33
Ridder, Hank, 50
Ridder, Joseph B., 7, 33, 35, 50, 52, 72-75
Ridder newspapers, 50

Robb, Arvin, 53
Roberts, John Griffith, 5
Robertsville, 1, 5
Robinson, Tony, x
Rockefeller, Nelson A., 45
Rockefeller family, 106
Rolla, Missouri, 91
Roma Bakery, 1
Romero Overlook, 20
Ronstadt, Linda, 25
Roos Bros., 60
Roosevelt, Franklin D., 3, 59, 89
Roosevelt, Theodore, 27, 28
Roosevelt Junior High School, 4
Rosa Street, 1, 3
Rosemary Gardens, 72-73
Rosicrucian Park, 41
Rotary Club, 25
Ruffo, Albert J., 7
Rushville, Indiana, 91
Ryan, Bob, 36
Rynhard, Armand, 90

Sacred Heart Novitiate, 10
Sainte Claire Hotel, 38
St. James Hotel, 26, 62
St. James Park, 27, 44, 47, 59, 68
St. John Street, 6
St. Patrick's Church, 94
St. Pius Church, Redwood City, 46
Salinger, Pierre, 12-13, 30
San Andreas Fault, 91, 92
San Augustine Street, 6
San Benito County, 44
San Bernardino *Sun*, 37
San Clemente, 32
Sandburg, Carl, 72
San Fernando Valley earthquake, 92
San Francisco *Call-Bulletin*, 37
San Francisco *Chronicle*, 12, 37, 40
San Francisco earthquake, 91, 92-96
San Francisco *Examiner*, 37, 45
San Francisco-Oakland Bridge, 91
San Gabriel Valley, 90
San Jose Chamber of Commerce, 107
San Jose Convention Center, 31
San Jose Country Club, 5
San Jose Foreign Trade Zone, 76
San Jose *Herald*, 28
San Jose High School, x, 89, 94
San Jose High School *Herald*, 38
San Jose Hospital, ix, 94
San Jose *Mercury*, 3n, 17, 23, 28, 35-42, 43, 46, 74
San Jose *Mercury Herald*, 3, 6, 35-42, 61, 69, 88, 105n, 106
San Jose *Mercury News*, 3n, 7, 21, 25, 33, 34, 35-42, 43, 44, 45, 48-52, 72, 75, 78, 88, 92, 101, 108
San Jose Municipal Airport, 3, 32, 47, 64
San Jose Municipal Stadium, 2
San Jose Museum of Art, 2, 93

San Jose *News*, x, 3n, 17, 35-42, 45, 46, 50, 54, 108
San Jose Public Library, 30, 93
San Jose State University, 6, 31, 33, 44, 46, 59, 66, 84-85, 89
    destruction of Quad, 70-71
    Tower Hall, 71
San Luis Dam, 20
San Quentin Prison, 57, 82
San Rafael, 77, 79
Santa Barbara, 88
Santa Clara, 94
Santa Cruz, 5, 14-15, 88, 90, 95
Santa Rosa, 93
Saratoga, 55, 95
Sauerwein, Mary Jeanne, 46
Sauliere, Frank, 54
Schlesinger, Arthur Jr., 46
Schmitz, Eugene, 95
Schroeder, Florence, 95-96
Seale, Bobby, 85, 86
Sheldon, Charles H., 23
Shockley, William, 18-20, 103, 107
Short, Walter C., 87
Shumway, DeVan L., 81
Signal Corps, U.S. Army, 106, 108
Silicon Valley, 1, 19, 76, 98, 101-108
Singapore, 101
Sirhan, Sirhan, 13
Smith, Walton Roland, 47
Sniadecki, Jim, 46
Solari, Louis, 66, 67, 89
Soledad Correctional Training Facility, 82
Soquel, 95
Soul on Ice, 82
Southern Pacific Railroad, 3, 4, 7, 11
Space Shuttle, 106
Spartan Daily, 44
Speer, Albert, 69
Spooner, William A., 45
Stallings, Bud, 45
Stanford, Leland, ix, x, 5
Stanford University, 5, 18, 27, 28, 46, 68, 101, 103, 106
Stassen, Harold, 21
State Board of Equalization, 15
State Capitol, x, 48-52, 60, 81-82
State Division of Forestry, 5
State Emergency Relief Administration (SERA), 3
State Legislature, x, 5, 15, 44, 48-52, 78, 81-82, 84
State Supreme Court, 16
Steffani, Ed, 64
Stevenson, Adlai, 13
Stockton, 3
Stokes, Art, 50
Sunnyvale, 13, 28, 29, 33, 90, 105, 107
Sunnyvale Air Base (Moffett Field), 103n, 105
Sunnyvale *Standard*, 24
Sutter, John, 20
"Swayback Hall," 59
Swift & Company, 72-76
Switzer, Gladys, 68

Tar Flat, 1, 4
Taylor Street, 6
Tehama County, 20
Telephone prefixes, 5-6
Temple Laundry, 107
Tetenbaum, Sid, 13
Thompson, John F. "Jack," 5, 15
Thorne, John, 13
Thurston family, 96
Tito, Josip Broz, 43
Tokyo, Japan, 101
Townsend, Calvin, 106, 108
Transamerica pyramid, 103
Trident missile, 106
Trounstine, Philip J., 66
Truman, Harry S., 10-11, 28-29
Truman, Margaret, 29
Tunney, John V., 31
TV Guide, 76

United for California, 50, 51
United States Supreme Court, 54n
University of California, 17, 28, 82, 92
University of the Pacific, 3
University of Pennsylvania, 107
University of Santa Clara, 10, 84, 93
Unruh, Jess, 48-52
USSR magazine, 108

Vacaville, 82
Valley Medical Center, 17
Varian, Russell, 106
Varian, Sigurd, 106
Varian Associates, 106
Vasconcellos, John, 47

Walker, Frank "Bunny," 56-57

Walker, Steven A., 57
Walt Disney Studios, 106
Ward, William, 66
Warner Communications, 107
Warren, Earl, 10-12, 39, 80, 87
Washington Post, 92
Washington School, 2
Watergate, 19, 32, 56
Watson, Fred, 66
Watson, Phil, 41
Watson, Thomas Jr., 107, 108
Watsonville, 13, 95
Webster Street, 6
Weinberger, Caspar W., 15-16
Weinstein, Linda, 92
Welch, Robert, 30, 31, 75
Western Appliance Co., 44
Westinghouse Electric Corporation, 28, 29
West Valley College, 84
Wheeler, Benjamin Ide, 28
White, Rosa, 3, 6
White, Thomas, 3
Whitney Street, 6
Willow Glen, 17, 42
Wilson, Lionel, 85
Wilson Junior High School, 1
Winchester, Sarah, ix
World Almanac, 93, 106
Worswick, G.D., 28, 95
Wright, Jack, 54

Young, Sharon, 97-99
Young, William, 95
Younger, Evelle, 45-46

Zertuche, Jose, 45